Fifty walks from
Haywards Heath

A handbook for seeking space in Mid Sussex

John Twisleton

Foreword by the Mayor of Haywards Heath

Illustrations by Rebecca Padgham

Commendations for
Fifty Walks from Haywards Heath

A very enjoyable collection of well-researched and well-described walks around the heart of mid-Sussex. It will direct even those who think they know Haywards Heath and its surrounding villages well into some new paths. The commentaries about some well-known local landmarks are worth the read on their own.

Sir James Dingemans

Having lived in Haywards Heath for all of my 70 years, with many happy childhood memories, and having seen so many changes transforming the town from a relatively small market town, to a bustling commuter town I particularly enjoyed this well researched book of walks.

Being something of a local historian, albeit in a very amateur capacity, I absolutely love the way the author has inextricably linked many of the walks with the history of Haywards Heath, covering the last 200 years or so.

My wife and I are avid walkers, and this book has shown us many footpaths, bridleways and places we had never visited before, and I would particularly commend it, not only to people who enjoy walking, but to those who would like to combine their walks with discovering more of our local history.

The walks vary from as little as a mile, to much longer walks for the more intrepid explorer, so in effect caters for most people. My wife and I have already thoroughly enjoyed participating in some of the walks, which are described very clearly and made easy to follow by the author.

Charles Tucker
Creator of Facebook Group 'Haywards Heath in days gone by'

Our town of Haywards Heath is so lucky to have the most amazing community spirit which, over the years, has been strengthened by people who are willing to spend a little time in their busy lives to 'do their bit' to bring fun and friendship to all. And this truly remarkable book, painstakingly researched by John is a great example of this - he shares such an array of interesting and diverse walks around our beautiful countryside for us all to enjoy.

As we all know, walking is one of the most beneficial aids to our health - and, particularly during the challenges of 'Lockdown', has proved the saving grace to many of us, both physically and mentally.

I commend this book to all who live in, and care for, our wonderful Town – and all the wonderful walks around it.

Ruth De Mierre
Mid Sussex District Councillor and Haywards Heath Town Team

St. Wilfrid's Church is adjacent to the Orchards Car Park where all walks commence, and as Church Warden I have been encouraged to explore some of the footpaths and by-ways selected by Canon John Twisleton.

The walks vary in length and therefore they are suitable for every age and ability. There is no fear of getting lost as every walk has the clearest of directions and the accompanying maps, although not detailed, display key features and landmarks to be found 'en route'.

During the Covid crisis we can all benefit from more physical exercise and experience the emotional enjoyment of our stunning local surroundings. The poetic and literary quotations provide thought for reflection and contemplation. The inclusion of historical and background information makes you exclaim "I didn't know that"! There are always hidden gems that lie in our immediate environment if only we knew where to look. With the help of this excellent guide you can discover them for yourself.

This book is certainly one to add to your library and if so, whether you do the walks on your own or with others, I am sure our paths will cross....

Arthur Franklin
Churchwarden of St Wilfrid, Haywards Heath

Copyright © 2020 John Twisleton
All rights reserved.
ISBN: 9798647040107

Foreword by the Mayor of Haywards Heath

We're so fortunate to all be able to enjoy such beautiful countryside around us in Mid Sussex. I spent my younger days at school at Hurst where the school year included trips to Danny and walks on the South Downs and beyond. As a school boy it was easy to take for granted our environs.

A few years on I now live in Haywards Heath with my family and still enjoy the history and local rambles around and about. At the time of writing we're in the first stages of coming out of Lockdown after ten weeks at home and doing our bit for the Covid-19 crisis. Being asked to write a foreword for this book couldn't have come at a better time. As part of our exercise routine we've walked and walked, discovering new tracks and footpaths and re-engaging with the outside world that we're so blessed to be part of. We've happened upon quite a few of the walks mentioned in this book such as through Ansty, Cuckfield and Blunts Wood and dipping into the book has sparked ideas of other new walks we can enjoy.

This collection of walks should be, I hope, something we can all relate to, drinking in our surroundings and hopefully coming out of these next few weeks and months with a renewed vigour for slowing down, appreciating a gentler pace of life, and fully appreciating the beauty and interest that is on our doorsteps.

Councillor Alastair McPherson,   October 2020

Contents

Title Page
Commendations
Copyright
Foreword
Introduction

Key to maps

1	Victoria Park	0.9 mile/1.5 kilometre
2	Muster Green	1 mile/1.7 km
3	Heath	1.2 mile/1.9 km
4	Dolphin	1.2 mile/2 km
5	Bolnore Village	1.2 mile/2 km
6	Beech Hurst	1.5 mile/2.5 km
7	Cemetery	1.5 mile/2.5 km
8	Southdowns Park	1.6 mile/2.5 km
9	Franklands Village	1.6 mile/2.5 km
10	Hospital	1.8 mile/2.9 km
11	Lindfield	1.8 mile/3.0 km
12	Mosque	1.9 mile/3.1 km
13	Wheatsheaf	2 mile/3.1 km
14	Beech Hurst	2.2 mile/3.6 km
15	Donald Campbell Plaque	2.7 mile/4.3 km
16	World's End	3 mile/4.9 km
17	Bolnore Village	3 mile/4.9 km
18	William Allen House	3.1 mile/5 km
19	Cuckfield	3.2 mile/5.1 km
20	Blunts Wood	3.2 mile/5.2 km
21	Scaynes Hill	3.7 mile/5.9 km
22	Wivelsfield Church	3.7 mile/6 km
23	Ansty	3.9 mile/6.2 km
24	Slugwash Lane	4.7 mile/7.5 km
25	Abbots Leigh	5.3 mile/8.5 km
26	Horsted Keynes	5.4 mile/8.6 km
27	Ardingly High Weald	5.4 mile/8.7 km
28	Lindfield	5.5 mile/8.9 km
29	Kenwards Farm	5.6 mile/9 kilometres
30	Cuckfield	5.6 mile/9 km
31	Walstead	5.8 mile/9.3 km
32	Ardingly College	6.5 mile/10.4 km
33	Wakehurst Place	6.7 mile/10.7 km
34	Ardingly Reservoir	6.9 mile/11.1 km
35	Heaven	7.8 mile/12.5 km
36	Balcombe	8 mile/12.9 km
37	Ditchling	8.3 mile/13.4 km
38	Borde Hill	8.3 mile/13.4 km
39	Scaynes Hill	8.6 mile/13.8 km

40	Birch Grove	8.6 mile/13.8 km
41	Paxhill Park	8.6 mile/13.9 km
42	Wivelsfield Church	8.8 mile/14.1 km
43	Buxshalls	8.9 mile/14.3 km
44	Plumpton Racecourse	9.2 mile/14.7 km
45	Ashdown Forest	9.5 mile/15.3 km
46	East Grinstead	9.6 mile/15.4 km
47	Ardingly	10.3 mile/16.6 km
48	Jack & Jill	11.4 mile/18.3 km
49	Brighton	13 mile/20.9 km
50	Lewes	13.1 mile/21.1 km

Notes
About the author

Introduction

One has to be alone, under the sky, before everything falls into place and one finds one's own place in the midst of it all, wrote Thomas Merton, making the connection between finding outer and inner space. The walks recorded here for your use were impelled by that recognition and by love of Haywards Heath and its surrounds. They were further fuelled by the Covid-19 pandemic which involved taking regular exercise with social distancing.

Fifty walks are listed in rough order of length from one mile up to thirteen. All start from Orchards shopping precinct car park RH16 3QH. Twenty three walks are circular. Twenty seven exploit public transport for the return journey. Through twenty years experience of living in Mid Sussex I have been able to write detailed walk routes with schematic illustrations to give an overall feel of them. Mainly based around the town with Cuckfield and Lindfield the walks extend radially to Balcombe, Ardingly, Horsted Keynes, Scaynes Hill, Wivelsfield, Ditching, Ansty and Borde Hill with longer excursions to East Grinstead, Lewes, Plumpton Racecourse and Brighton.

As a volunteer member of Haywards Heath Town Team I am active in promoting a deeper grasp of town history which has served to illustrate this book. Most chapters draw out points of interest or amusement about the walk route. Each walk has an inspirational saying, drawn from a variety of sources including Sussex poets, to serve seeking 'oxygen of the spirit' on the walk replenishing the inner space that helps bring us fully alive.

Walking on public footpaths brings with it responsibility to respect surrounding land in private ownership especially farmland and to take special care when passing livestock.

The book provides acknowledgement of local authors who inform it. I would like to thank James Twisleton, Dave Twisleton-Ward and Anne Twisleton for their help and most especially Rebecca Padgham for assisting with the illustrations.

Canon Dr John F Twisleton   **October 2020**

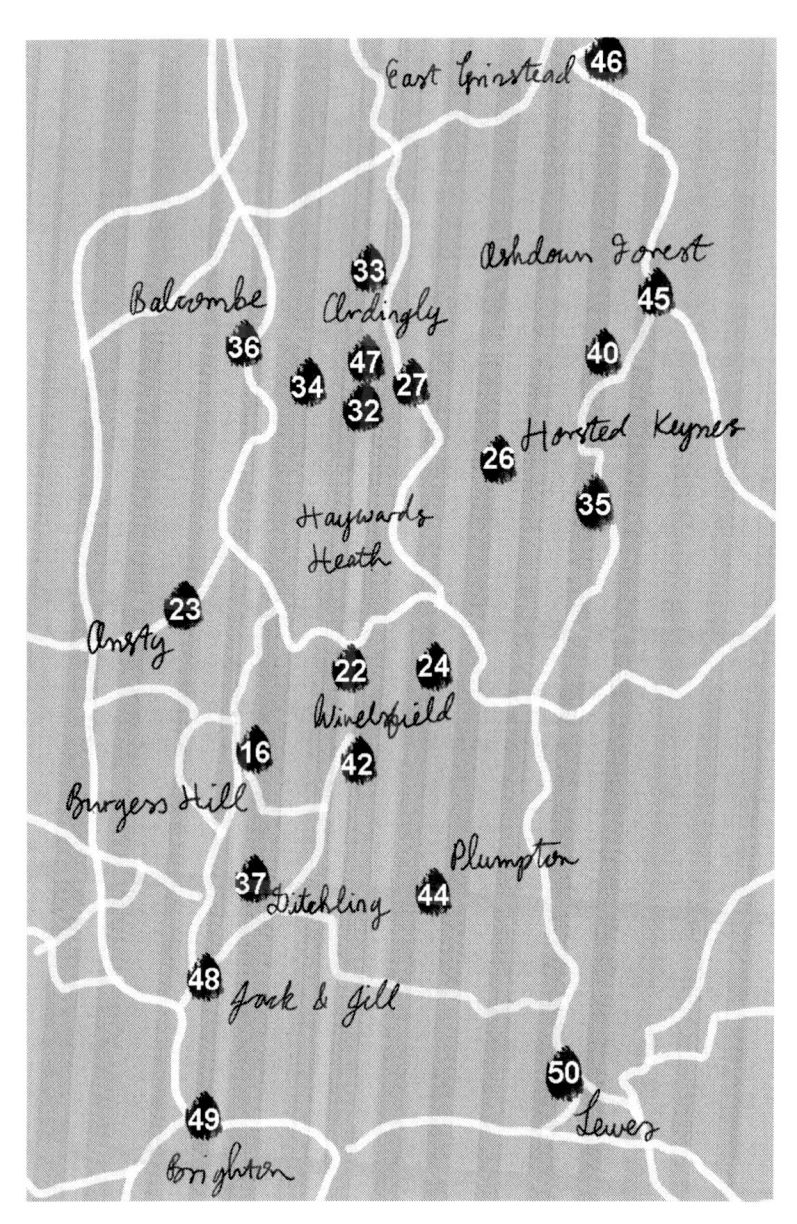

Map key: Haywards Heath and Mid Sussex

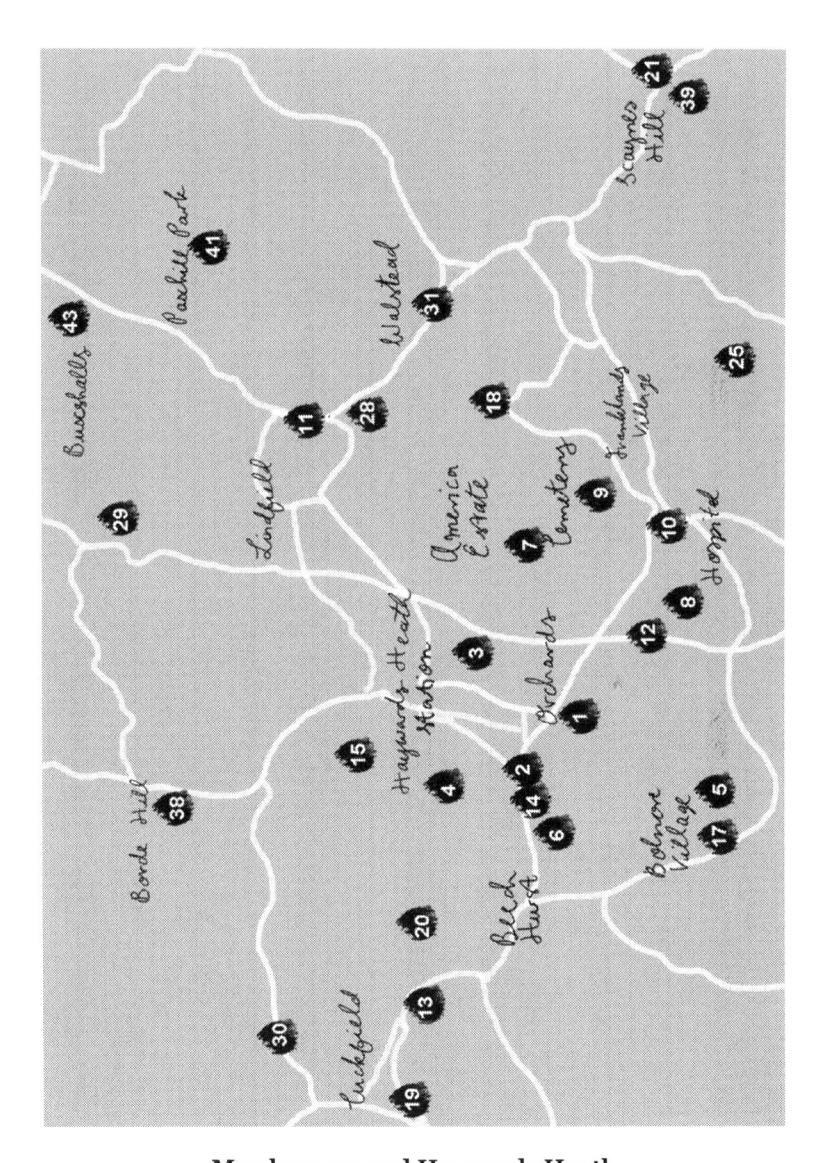

Map key: around Haywards Heath

1 Victoria Park

> 1 mile walk through Orchards precinct along South Road and around Victoria Park returning via scenically situated St Wilfrid's parish church

We must live life less as an attempt to conquer new land and hold on to it and more as a grateful response to the gifts of God. Henri Nouwen

Haywards Heath residents value the Orchards shopping precinct which is partly weather proofed and has five pay and display car parks around it as well as places you can park for free if you stay for a short period. It's a community hub. At holiday time there is entertainment laid on for families which helps make the precinct even more of a hub. Orchards grew in the shadow of St Wilfrid's Church central to the town and to Chichester Diocese which covers Sussex.

Walk down the precinct and turn right following the pavement to the pedestrian crossing before Victoria Park. Cross and turn right along the pavement and then left to enter the park walking clockwise towards the cafeteria. Enjoy the view of St Wilfrid's. The embankment followed by the path returning to South Road was built from earth excavated to make the railway tunnel opened 1840. Cross South Road and ascend the steps into the old cemetery to walk up to the main door of St Wilfrid's on Church Road pausing to look back and take in the view of the South Downs. You may like to tour the Church built by George Bodley 1863-5 to serve the community created by the arrival of the railway. Bodley's creation towers over Haywards Heath and is striking in its noble simplicity. Return along Church Road and turn right down St Wilfrid's Way to Orchards car park.

0.9 mile/1.5 km

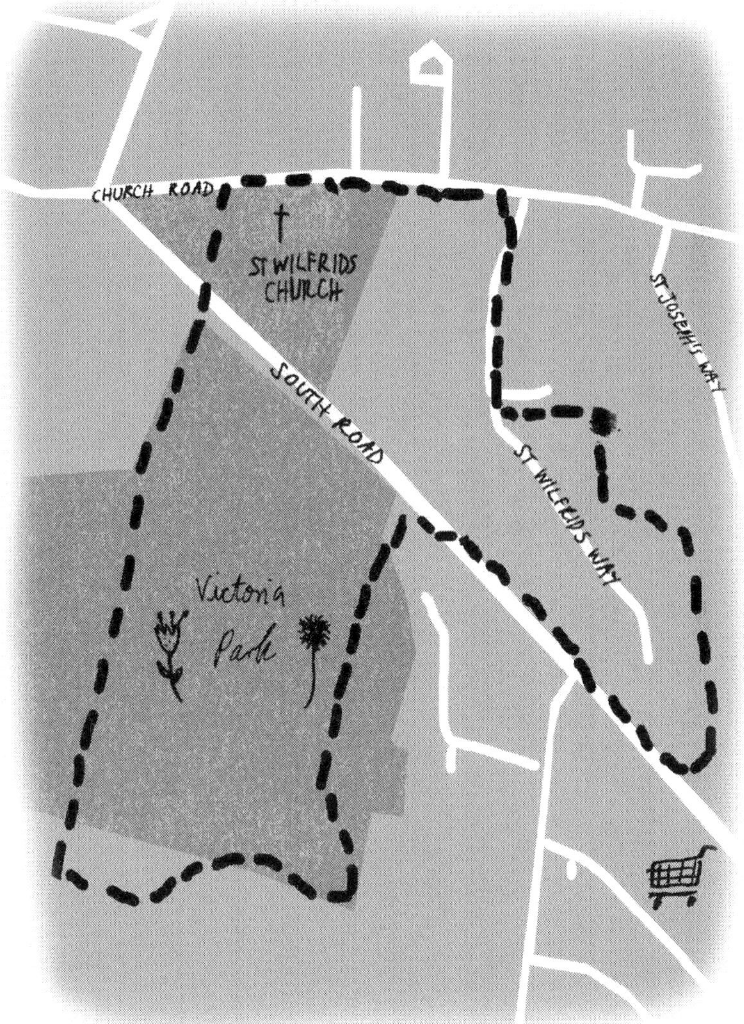
CHURCH ROAD
ST WILFRIDS CHURCH
SOUTH ROAD
ST WILFRIDS WAY
ST JOSEPH'S WAY
Victoria Park

Muster Green

> Circular walk around the old centre of Hayward's Heath

If I ever become a rich man, or ever I grow to be old, I will build a house with deep thatch to shelter me from the cold, And there shall the Sussex songs be sung and the story of Sussex told. Hilaire Belloc

The battle of Haywards Heath in 1642 brought Royalists from Chichester to arms against Puritan Lewes folk allegedly on Muster Green one of the oldest sites in Haywards Heath shown on a map of 1638 and now site of our war memorial. The Roundhead victory was a turning point in the English Civil War denying King Charles I's forces access to Lewes and south coast ports. Originally the mustering at Muster Green on Haywards Heath was of pigs rather than troops as permitted by a thirteenth century charter.

From the Orchards car park head east across St Wilfrid's Way, through Centenary Hall car park continuing through the churchyard to Church Rd. Turn left past the Church down to Zizzi's restaurant and cross the Gyratory to The Star Pub. Turn right and follow the pavement. Cross the road again and turn left to walk over the top of the railway tunnel. You can see the tunnel ventilator on the other side of the road. Walk across the top of Boltro Road and cross to Muster Green. 'Boltro' is short for 'bull trough', a reminder of how that road was principal access for cattle walked to the market by the station in earlier days. Walk the length of the Green to the war memorial opposite the Miller & Carter Steakhouse. A building is recorded on this site on the 1638 map. Cross Muster Green South road and continue left on the pavement, back past the Gyratory to the shops and through Orchards precinct to the car park.

1 mile/1.7 km

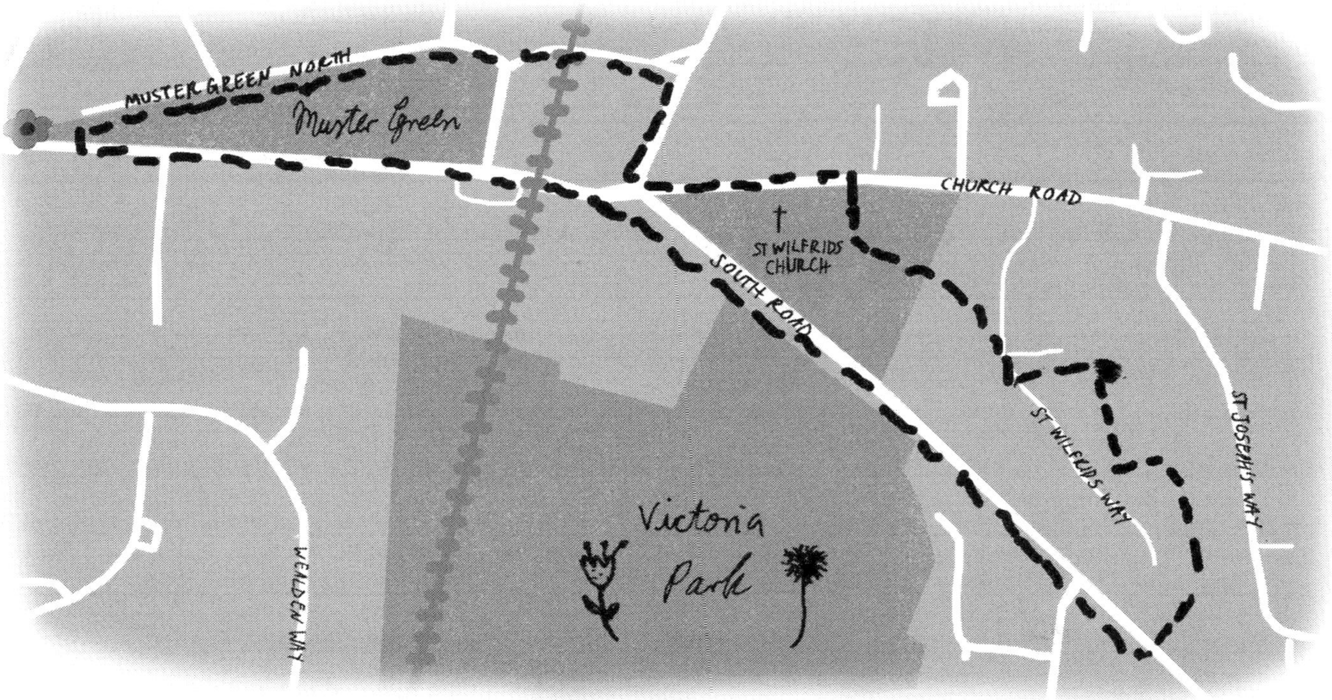

MUSTER GREEN NORTH
Muster Green
CHURCH ROAD
ST WILFRIDS CHURCH
SOUTH ROAD
ST WILFRIDS WAY
ST JOSEPH'S WAY
Victoria Park
WEALDEN WAY

3   Heath

> 1 mile circular walk around the ancient heath aka Clair Park

We who have lived before railways were made belong to another world. Stage-coaches, more or less swift, riding-horses, pack-horses, highwaymen and so forth - all these belong to the old period. But your railroad starts the new era. Thackeray

Nasty experiences with highwaymen on Haywards Heath, the 'hoth' or wasteland outside Cuckfield and Lindfield, are part of folklore to the extent of the seeming invention of a fearsome Jack Hayward who once ruled it to whom you had to 'stand and deliver'! This romantic legend got under the collar of a Rector of St Wilfrid's who put in an unsuccessful bid to rename the new town 'St Wilfrid's'. The legend is dispatched by references to Hayworth Hoth going back to the 13th century. Hayworth derives from old English words about an enclosure of land and there is 17th century evidence for this enclosing.

From Orchards car park head north to Church Road, cross and follow the footpath next to the carpark, into Trevelyan Place. At Heath Road, cross and follow the footpath descending through the residue of the ancient heath to the Cricket Pavilion across from the railway station which opened in 1841. The arrival of the railway made for the growth of Haywards Heath as a town since, with the adjacent A23, it opened up the possibility of living in the attractive heart of Sussex whilst travelling to lucrative work in London, Brighton, Crawley and Gatwick airport. Each morning and evening the heath sees a busy flow of commuters heading to and from the railway station. Continue your circuit of the heath returning the way you came via the footpaths to Church Road and Orchards.

1.2 miles/1.9 km

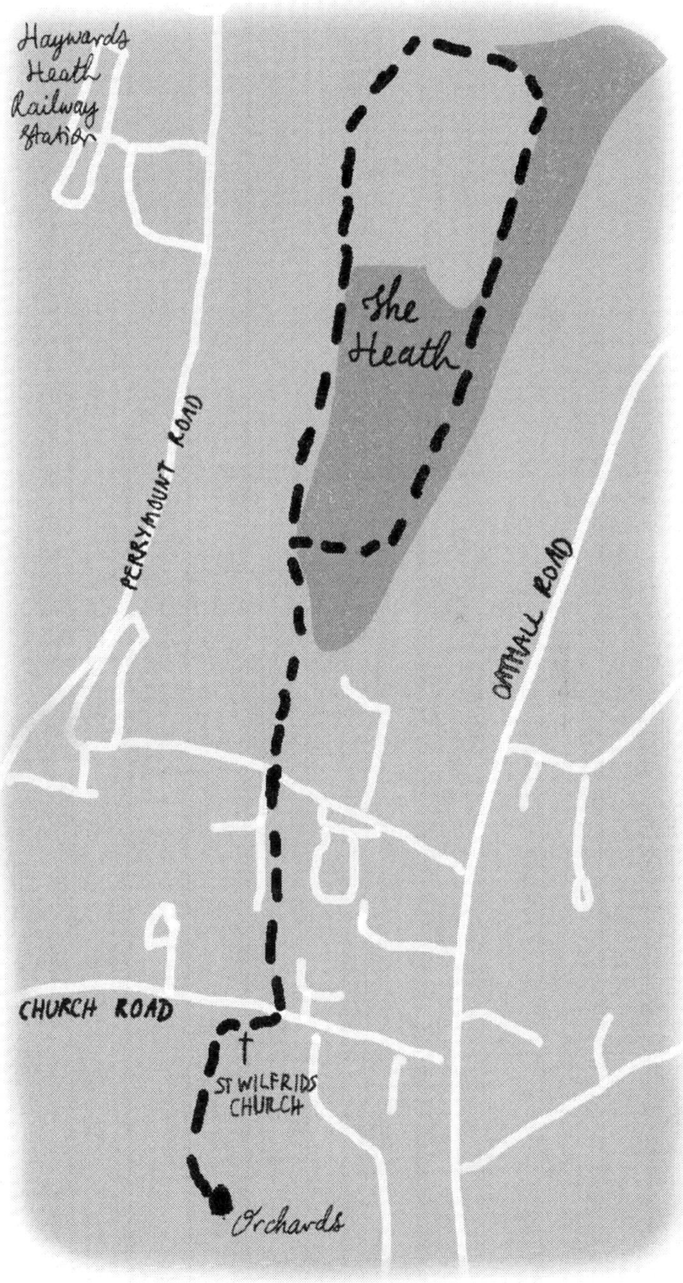
Haywards Heath Railway Station
The Heath
PERRYMOUNT ROAD
OATHALL ROAD
CHURCH ROAD
ST WILFRIDS CHURCH
Orchards

4 Dolphin

> 1 mile walk to the Dolphin Leisure Centre returning by bus

Humans think they are smarter than dolphins because we build cars and buildings and start wars etc., and all that dolphins do is swim in the water, eat fish and play around. Dolphins believe that they are smarter for exactly the same reasons. Douglas Adams

The Dolphin Leisure Centre is a social hub for Haywards Heath. Its name is a reminder of how the town grew from Cuckfield after the railway appeared in 1840. The Sergison family of Cuckfield had enormous influence tracing back to Commissioner of the Navy Charles Sergison who was resident at Cuckfield Place from 1693 until his death in 1732. His shield has three dolphins on it. Because Haywards Heath grew out of Cuckfield the Sergison dolphin symbol was chosen for the town's Sports Centre. Dolphins, being friendly creatures, are signs of peace and harmony.

Head north from Orchards car park to Church Road, cross and follow the footpath next to the carark, into Trevelyan Place. At Heath Road, cross and follow the footpath descending through the ancient heath aka Clair Park to the Cricket Pavilion, exiting at the top onto Perrymount Road. Turn right, crossing before the roundabout then walking past Haywards Heath Station under the railway bridge continuing past the station back entrance. Cross right at the traffic island before the Boltro Road sign, continue along and cross onto the island with the Cuckfield sign on it. Cross again to the top of Milton Road to follow the signed footpath down towards the rear of the Dolphin Leisure Centre. Take the path on your right down and round to the entrance on Pasture Hill Rd. Turn right, then right into Harlands Road, crossing with care at the traffic island to follow the road to Sainsbury's bus stop. Catch a 30, 31, 39 or 166 bus back to Orchards or return via the Cricket Pavilion.

1.2 miles/2 km

Sainsbury's

Dolphin Centre

Haywards Heath Railway Station

Cricket Pavilion

HEATH ROAD

Orchards Car Park

5   Bolnore Village

> 1 mile walk across Victoria Park through Ashenground woods to Bolnore village returning by bus

The real voyage of discovery consists not in seeking new landscapes but in having new eyes. Marcel Proust

Housing is a hot potato in Sussex with so much beautiful countryside protected from development by law. In the late 1990s permission for expanding Haywards Heath to the south west was granted with the first houses in Bolnore Village completed 2002. Since the Ashenground and Catts Woods were a Site of Nature Conservation Interest this development was controversial. As a condition the developers had to build Haywards Heath by-pass as a relief road benefiting the town. This re-routing of the A272 was completed in 2014. A striking 1638 map published by Haywards Heath Society was used in Stuart Meier's 2006 submission to the Bolnore Village Planning Inquiry as evidence 'that certain wooded parcels have ancient woodland continuity, and the effects of development should be mitigated in an appropriate manner'. How much that was achieved can be judged on this walk.

Our walk to Bolnore Village starts by descending the Orchards precinct and turning right along the pavement to the pedestrian crossing. Cross and turn right along the pavement then left to enter Victoria Park. Walk diagonally across to exit the bottom south west corner into Drummond Close. Walk along the Close then turn right proceeding down Sunnywood Drive to the first junction. Turn right into the ancient Ashenground Road (here named Keymer End) which provides access into the woods of that name. After crossing the railway bridge turn sharp left and walk on the path nearest to the railway until you see the small bridge on the right. Cross and follow the pathway through the trees into the village. Behind the Market Square, catch a 33 or 39 bus back to Orchards.

1.2 mile/2 km

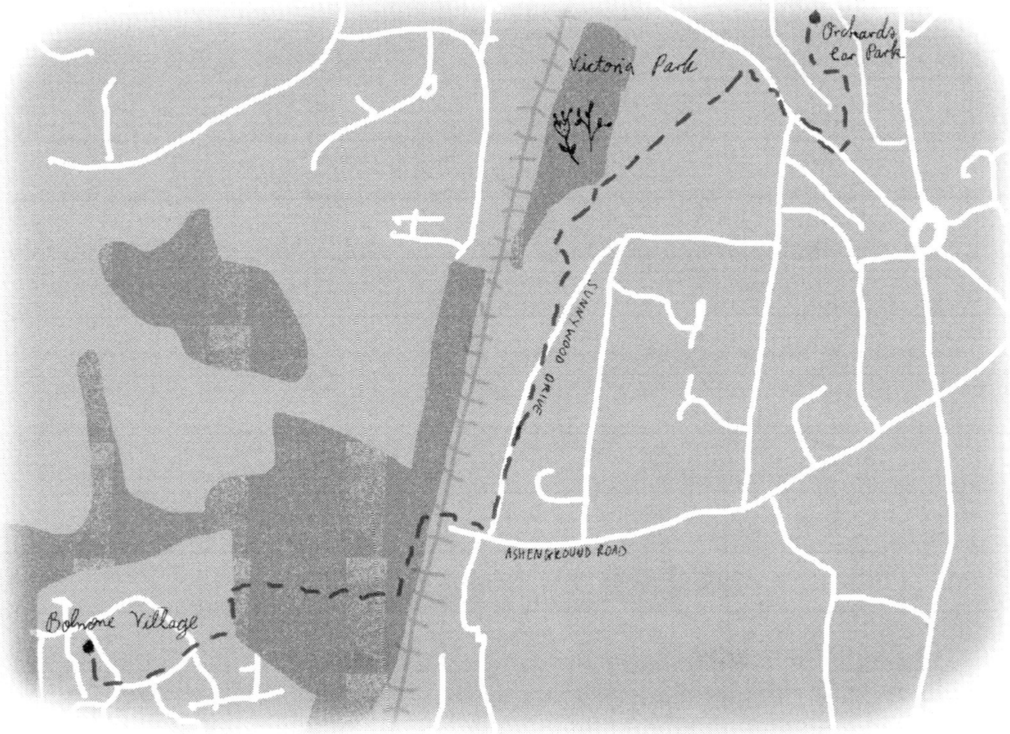
Orchards Car Park
Victoria Park
SUNNYWOOD DRIVE
Bolmore Village

6   Beech Hurst

> 2 mile circular walk to a scenic park popular on account of its miniature railway

I never get between the pines, but I smell the Sussex air, nor I never come on a belt of sand but my home is there; and along the sky the line of the Downs so noble and so bare. Hilaire Belloc

Beech Hurst with its fabulous grounds overlooking the South Downs is the pride of Haywards Heath. The original house, demolished in the 1950s, was inhabited by Mr W J Yapp who gifted the estate to the town. In the 1914-18 war it was a hospital annexe for military patients. The miniature railway open seasonally has a half mile track with views over the Downs and features two tunnels, steaming bays where the engines are prepared and a signalling system.

Head from the Orchards car park east across St Wilfrid's Way, through Centenary Hall car park continuing through the churchyard to Church Rd. Turn left past the Church down to Zizzi's restaurant, site of the Church of England school for 90 years. With comings and goings across the road The Star Pub opposite held prominence at what was then the busy town centre. This centre shifted to South Road when the school moved to Eastern Road in 1951. At the junction, cross South Road using the left pelican crossing. Turn right and follow the pavement across from Muster Green to the two roundabouts by the War Memorial and the Police Station. At the second roundabout cross Bolnore Road and continue straight ahead. After the pelican crossing, turn left to enter the Beechurst Estate, enjoying the railway and the splendid view of the South Downs. Return the way you came, past the Police Station, but at Zizzi's continue on the South Road pavement. Take the pedestrian crossing after Victoria Park, turn left along the pavement then right up the cutting to Orchards car park.

1.5 mile/2.5 km

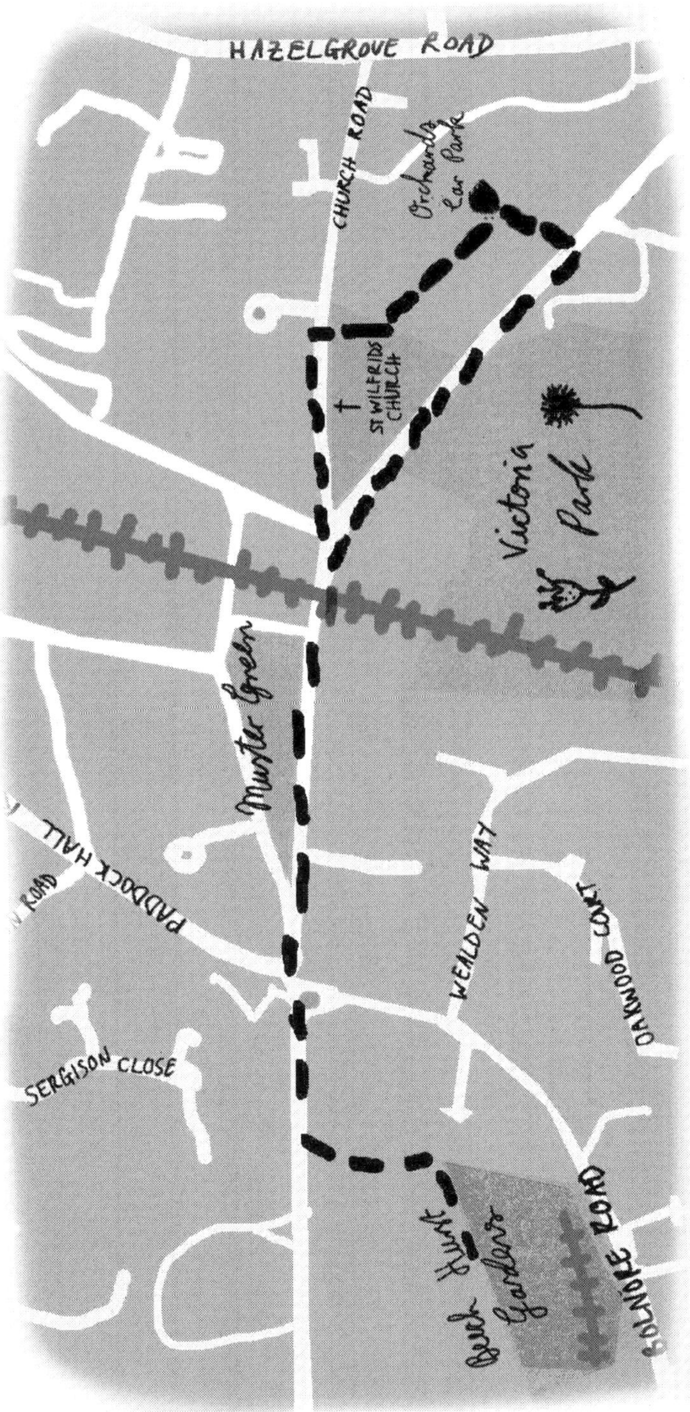
HAZELGROVE ROAD
CHURCH ROAD
Orchards Car Park
ST WILFRIDS CHURCH
Victoria Park
Muster Green
PADDOCK HALL
ROAD
WEALDEN WAY
OAKWOOD COURT
SERGISON CLOSE
BOLNORE ROAD
Beech Hurst Gardens

7   Cemetery

> 2 mile circular walk past The Priory to the Cemetery and Presentation Church in America Estate

Without faith we will never understand the source of our own love and goodness and without doubt we will infect them with our prejudice and partiality. Lionel Blue

An octogenarian recalling his youth in Haywards Heath during the 1960s reflects on the rather severe dominance of the walled convent near the town centre. He recalls there being the occasional appearance of one nun pushing another in a wheelchair. By then the Priory of Our Lady of Good Counsel founded 1886 had dwindled as a community. The Order relinquished the Priory in 1977 and many walls came down to serve local housing development. The splendid building converted into flats remains a notable feature on the skyline.

From Orchards car park descend through the precinct and turn left along South Road. Continue down to the roundabout and turn left down Caxton Way continuing straight ahead down the Syresham Gardens footpath beside the stream to St Augustine's Way. Turn right then left along Priory Way to Western Road. Turn left and after North Road, cross the road to enter the town's scenic Cemetery. Town growth required expansion from St Wilfrid's cemetery in 1917. After walking around the cemetery, continue up Western Road to New England Road crossing to the right to view Presentation Church (1886) donated by philanthropist Mary Otter to serve the America Estate named after another philanthropist, William Allen whose allotment colony served the poor of this area from 1820. From Presentation Church head back uphill along New England Road. Cross Hazelgrove Road at the top, turn right then left into Church Road to return to Orchards.

1.5 mile/2.5km

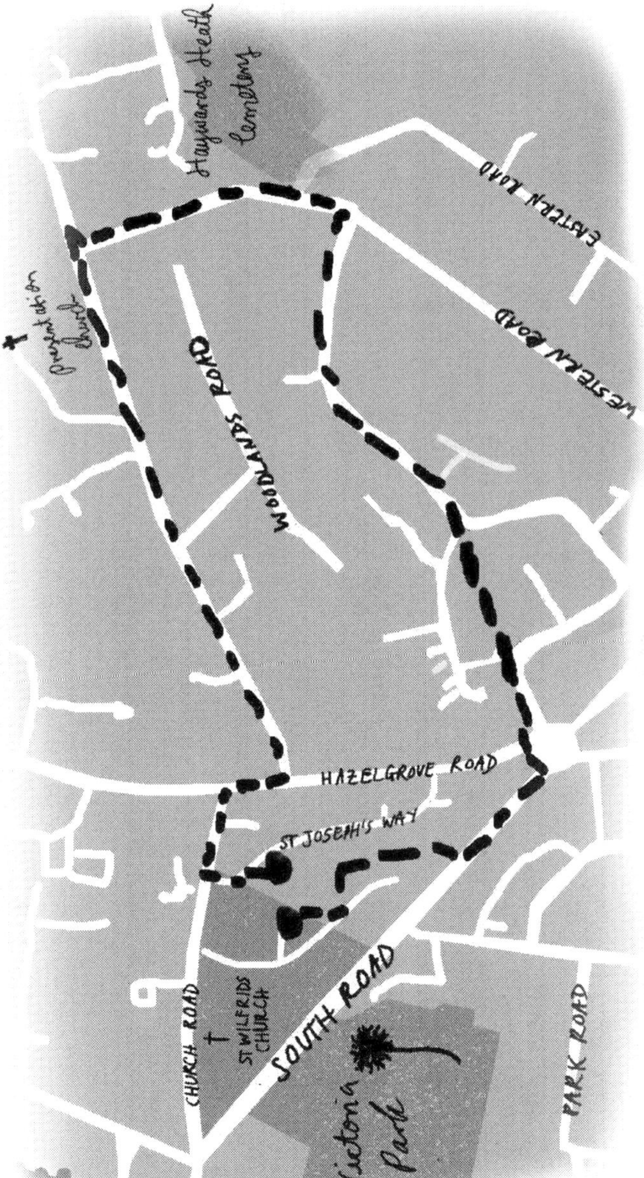

Haywards Heath Cemetery
EASTERN ROAD
WESTERN ROAD
Presentation Church
WOODLANDS ROAD
HAZELGROVE ROAD
ST JOSEPH'S WAY
ST WILFRIDS CHURCH
CHURCH ROAD
SOUTH ROAD
PARK ROAD
Victoria Park

8   Southdowns Park

> 2 mile circular walk to the scenic old hospital buildings overlooking Haywards Heath and the South Downs

What mental health needs is more sunlight, more candour, and more unashamed conversation. Glenn Close

The railway's arrival in Haywards Heath at the centre of Sussex made it the obvious venue for what was initially called the County Lunatic Asylum constructed during the 1850s. The hospital, designed by Henry Kendall in Italianate style with corridor layout, became known after the introduction of the National Health Service as St Francis Hospital. Treatment of mental illness in Victorian times differs so much from our day, with isolation seen as the key for fear almost of contamination. Haywards Heath Asylum broke new ground in treating mental illness through pioneer Doctor Lockhart Robertson who used vapour baths to soothe his patients. The population of Haywards Heath in 1883 was 1,814 but this figure excluded roughly the same number in the colony south east of the town which had its own farm. The creation of the hospital south of the town made Haywards Heath the shape it is, reaching down south east from Cuckfield to Wivelsfield without an obvious centre. The story of the asylum converted into the apartments at Southdowns Park is told in 'Sweet bells jangled out of tune' by James Gardner (1999).

From Orchards car park walk down through the shopping precinct, cross at the crossing and turn left along South Road. At the roundabout cross Sussex Road, to take the 3rd exit, Franklynn Rd. Continue along then turn right into Triangle Rd, and immediately left to proceed up Kents Road into the path at the top of the road into Colwell Gardens leading to Colwell Road. After touring the estate across the road with its splendid view of the South Downs re-enter Colwell Road. Turn left to return to Orchards via Wivelsfield Road which gives way to Sussex Road and, after the roundabout, South Road.

1.6 mile/2.5km

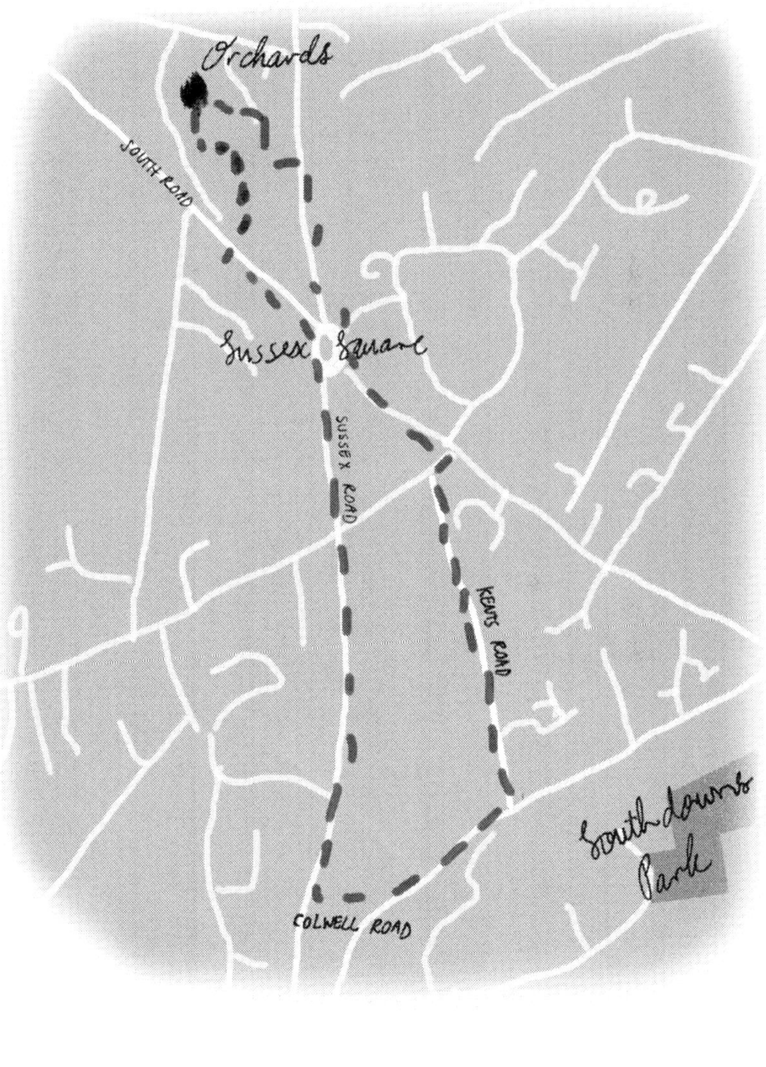

Orchards
SOUTH ROAD
Sussex Square
SUSSEX ROAD
KEATS ROAD
Southdowns Park
COLWELL ROAD

9   Franklands Village

> 2 mile walk to Franklands Village via the America Estate returning by bus

Service above self. Rotary Club motto

The growth of Haywards Heath was impacted by the 1930s depression when worst unemployment was in the building industry. At that time Rotary International opened a local branch. After research they initiated the building of Franklands Village on 45 acres of land to the east of the town 'covered with heavy scrub and large trees and somewhat hilly, but seeming to offer a suitable site for building'. This philanthropy addressed both unemployment and the lack of homes suitable for renting by young couples. Architect Harold Turner (1885-1961) born in Ardingly designed the Village. The curly gutter brackets on houses in Haywards Heath are his trademark 'Arts and Crafts' twist on the traditional Sussex farmhouse.

From Orchards head east across the car park, then right down St Joseph's Way to Hazelgrove Road. Cross to the Roman Catholic Church built 1928 in the Priory convent grounds, Romanesque with an icon of its patron St Paul above the door. Continue down to the roundabout and turn left down Caxton Way continuing straight ahead down the Syresham Gardens footpath beside the stream to St Augustine's Way. Turn right then left along Priory Way to Western Road. Turn left and cross the road into the Cemetery. Walk down to the bottom, turn right and exit onto a path through the wood, and at the footpath junction turn left to ascend the tarmac slope. Cross the road taking the footpath ahead to enter Franklands Village recreation ground. Turn right when you reach Gravelye Lane, heading past the village shop onto Northlands Avenue. Turn right, right again at the roundabout, crossing at the pelican opposite Princess Royal Hospital and catch a bus back to Orchards (30, 31, 33, 39, 62, 89, 166, 270, 271, 272 or 769).

1.6 mile/2.5km

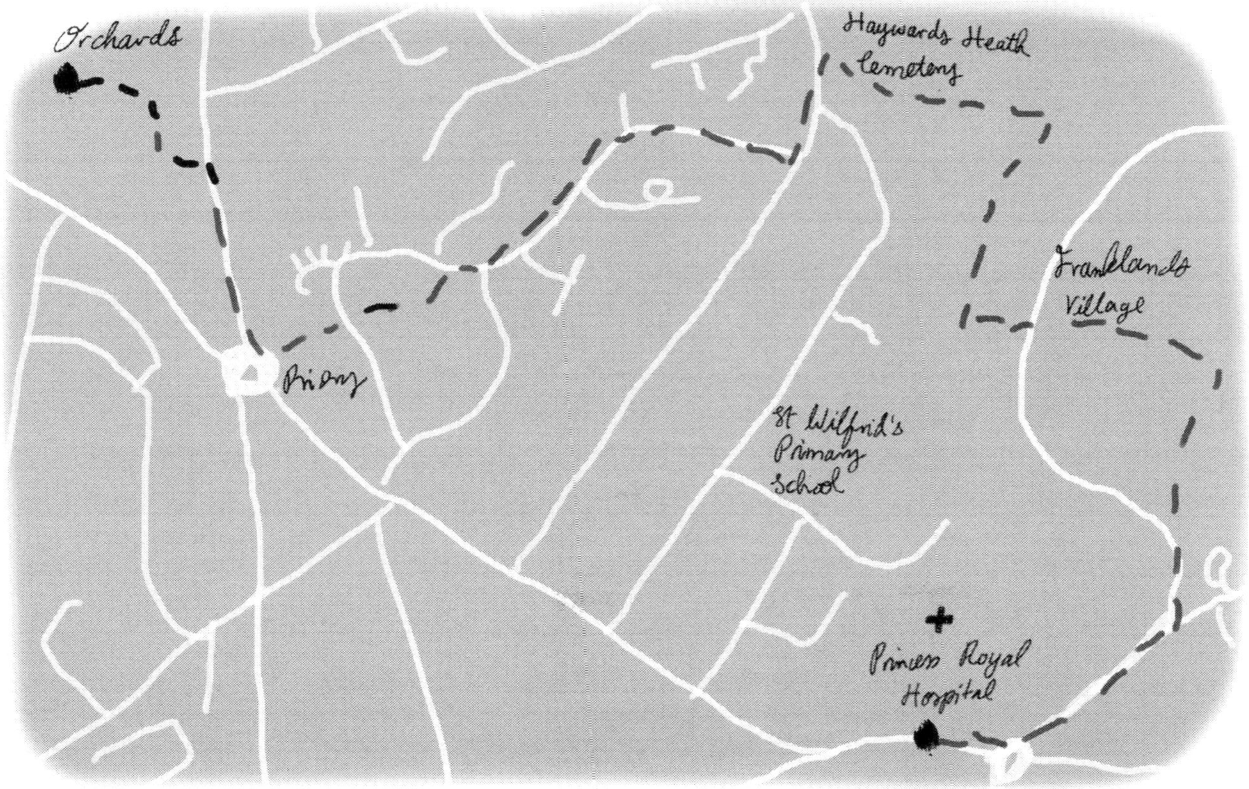
Orchards
Haywards Heath Cemetery
Priory
Franklands Village
St Wilfrid's Primary School
Princess Royal Hospital

Hospital

> 2 mile circular walk to Princess Royal Hospital

It is health that is real wealth and not pieces of gold and silver. Gandhi

One of the riches of Haywards Heath is its hospital opened 1991 by Princess Anne. Standing on the site of a former mental hospital Princess Royal Hospital is the main hospital in Mid Sussex and part of the Brighton and Sussex University Hospitals NHS Trust with patients coming and going between Haywards Heath and Brighton. Hospital patients based in the wards on upper floors are able to enjoy a beautiful view of the South Downs. Town residents help supply a good number of hospital volunteers. The Princess Royal is served by no less than eleven buses which makes it a hub for Mid Sussex walkers.

From Orchards car park descend through the shopping precinct, cross at the crossing and turn left at South Road. At the roundabout cross Sussex Road, to take the 3rd exit, Franklynn Rd. Continue along, observing the Priory building, former Roman Catholic convent on the opposite side of the road. Turn right into Triangle Rd, and immediately left to proceed up Kents Road, past the Christian Meeting Hall of that name linked to the Plymouth Brethren. At the top of the road is a short path to Colwell Gardens leading to Colwell Road. Turn left and walk along to the junction with Franklynn Road. Take a right turn and right again at the bus stop into the grounds of the hospital. Walk down beside the car park to the hospital buildings and turn left for the entrance, shop and cafeteria. Return to the bus stop heading left down Franklynn Road to the roundabout. Bear left, cross South Road and walk to your right past the shops to cross back into Orchards.

1.8 mile/2.9km

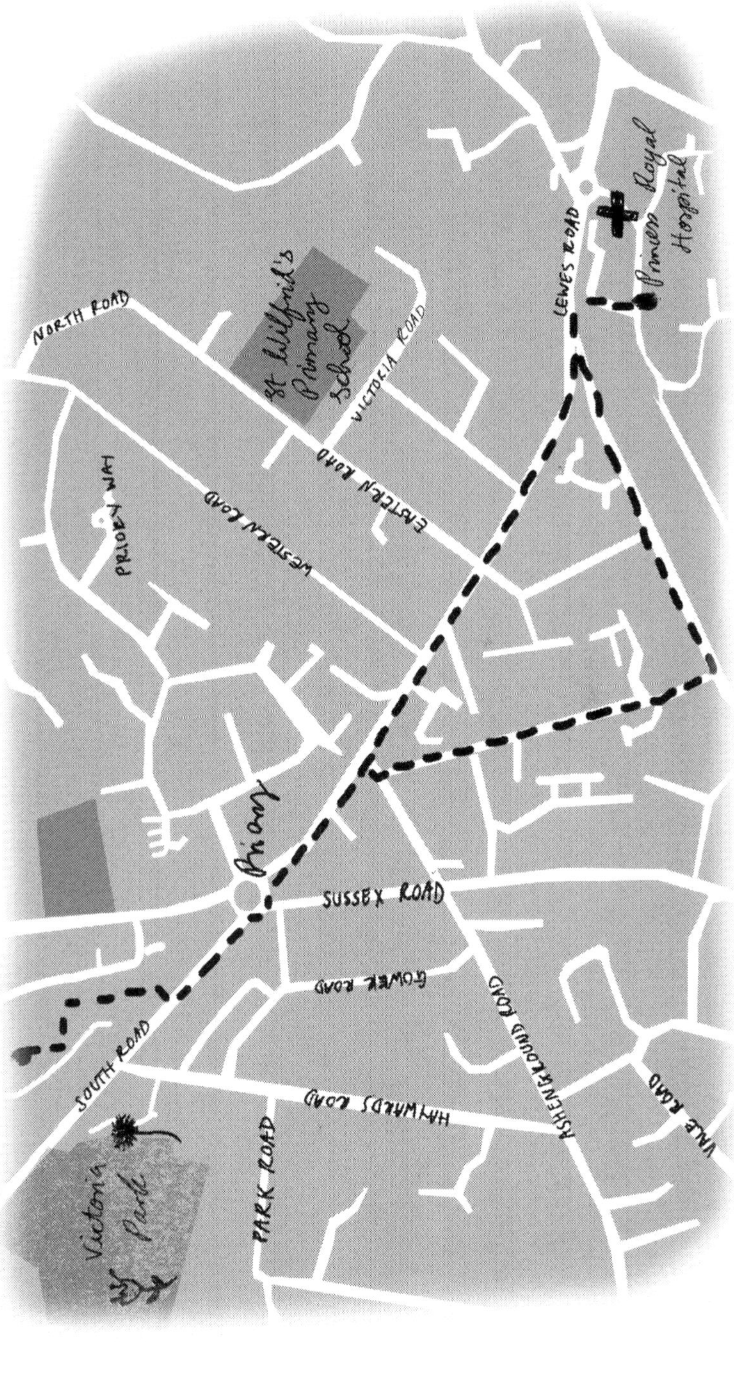

NORTH ROAD
St Wilfrid's Primary School
VICTORIA ROAD
EASTERN ROAD
WESTERN ROAD
PRIORY WAY
LEWES ROAD
Princess Royal Hospital
Priory
SUSSEX ROAD
GOWER ROAD
ASHENGROUND ROAD
SOUTH ROAD
HAYWARDS ROAD
VALE ROAD
PARK ROAD
Victoria Park

11   Lindfield

> 2 mile walk to the ancient village of Lindfield returning by bus

The serene beauty of a holy life is the most powerful influence in the world. Pascal

The railway arrived by agreement at a distance from Lindfield bringing with it workers to build what became Haywards Heath. Canny management of Lindfield's Stand Up Pub, opened in the 1840s, provided no chairs to assist turnover and deter workers from lingering over their ale, hence the name. Through local Quaker philanthropist William Allen (1770-1843) Lindfield had already contributed to what was to become Haywards Heath. Allen established a 'colony' for agricultural workers off Gravelye Lane. 'Colony' then had association with 'America'. Allen's project is recalled by the street names in America estate.

From Orchards car park head up to Church Road and turn right. Cross Hazelgrove Road and turn right heading left down New England Road in the America estate. After the shops turn left along Barn Cottage Lane with the recreation ground to your right. Cross Hanbury Lane and continue down the path between the houses into Scrase Valley Local Nature Reserve. After 200 yards turn right at the junction and follow Scrase stream on your left. At one point you duck under a large pipe. Exit the Reserve into Croxton Lane keeping the stream to your left and cross the bridge on the advertised public footpath into Meadow Drive. Cross the Drive to continue on the footpath opposite which leads to the tennis courts at the southern corner of Lindfield Common recreation ground. Continue diagonally across the field to enter Lindfield High Street. Opposite the Stand Up Pub you can catch a 30, 270 or 272 bus back to Orchards Precinct.

1.8 mile/3km

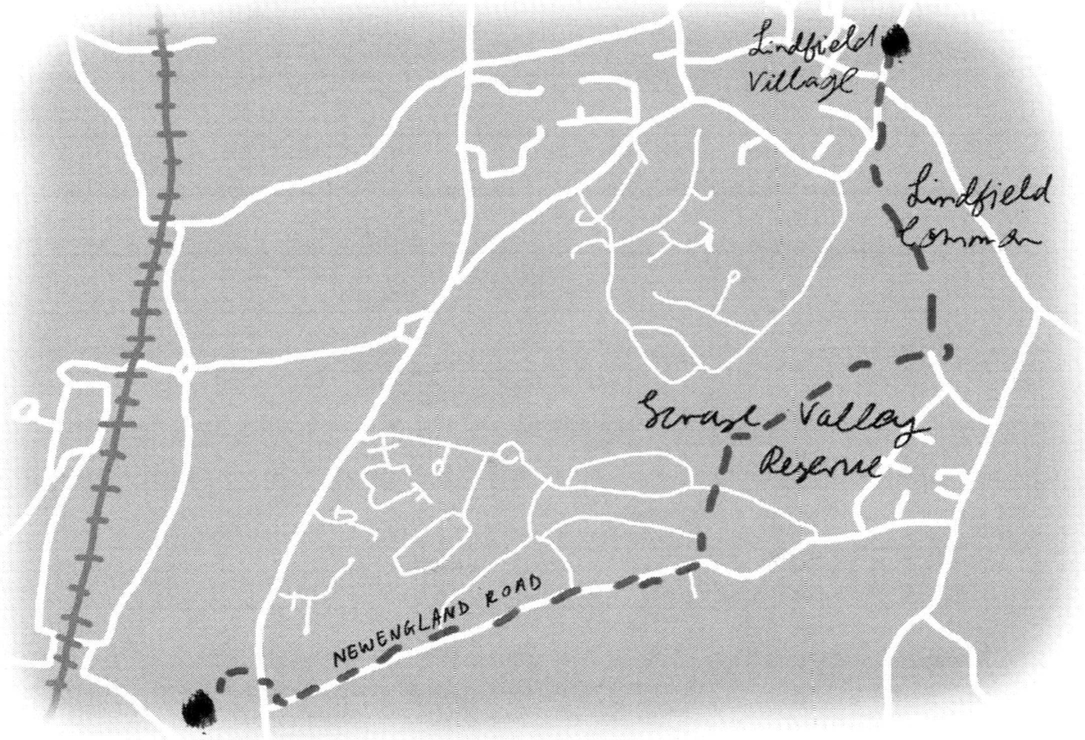
Lindfield Village
Lindfield Common
Scrase Valley Reserve
NEWENGLAND ROAD

12   Mosque

> 2 mile circular walk round the town visiting the Mosque and Ascension Church

There will be no peace among the nations without peace among religions. There will be no peace among religions without dialogue among religions. Hans Küng

The second Church of the Ascension in Vale Road was dedicated 1966. The first was an iron building in St John's Road erected 1895 'to cater for the Asylum area taken over from Wivelsfield'. It was demolished and the congregation re-sited as St Edmund's Church at the former Congregational Church on Wivelsfield Road moving on later to the new build Ascension Church. They left a building now serving as Haywards Heath Islamic Centre with a gallery assisting separation of men and women in Muslim worship. This history and its associated walk reveal something of church development and the diversification of faith in the town over the last century.

From the car park descend through Orchards shopping precinct and cross South Road at the pedestrian crossing. Turn left and walk down past the roundabout into Sussex Road. Across the road you will see the recently rebuilt Baptist Church and, after Triangle Road, the Jireh Strict Baptist Church. Beyond that your eye will be caught by the white painted Mosque open daily for prayer. After viewing the Mosque we head for where its former congregation settled by turning right into Edward Road and then left into Vale Road where Ascension Church will come into view. Continue past the Church curving right into Sheppeys. After passing the entrance to Ashenground Wood proceed up Sunnywood Drive. Turn left at Drummond Close then walk across Victoria Park with its view of St Wilfrid's, mother Church of the Ascension, and turn right for Orchards.

1.9 mile/3.1km

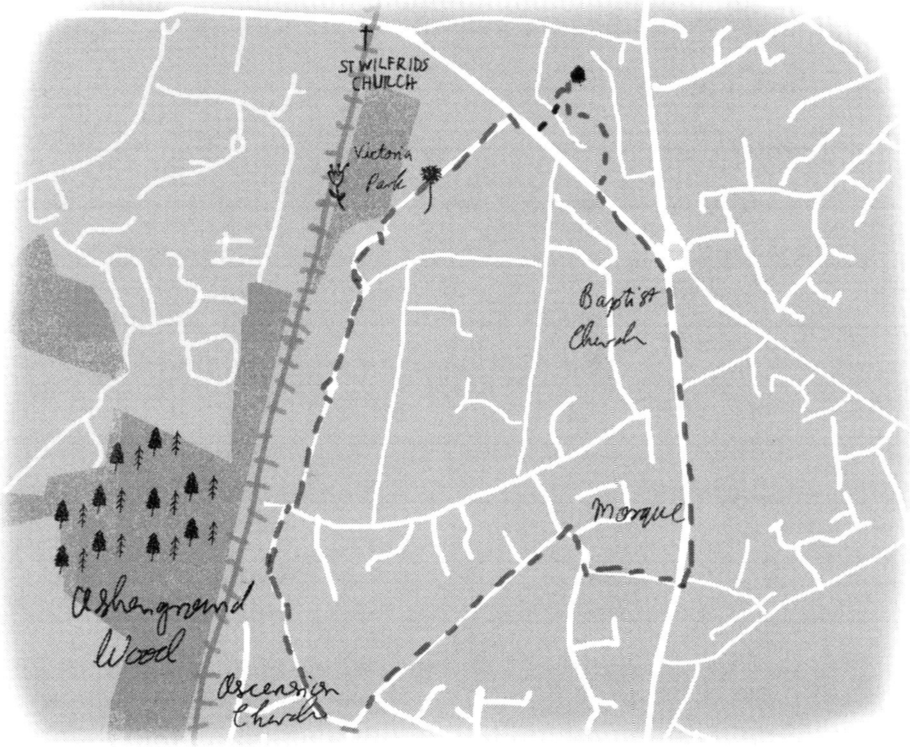
ST WILFRIDS CHURCH
Victoria Park
Baptist Church
Mosque
Ashenground Wood
Ascension Church

13 Wheatsheaf

> Sussex is famous for its woodland. Haywards Heath residents enjoy walking 2 miles to the Wheatsheaf Pub through Blunts Wood and catching a bus back to town

Sussex is enchanted land! It lives within the heart although the lover and his love have long since dwelt apart. But the hidden dreams, the singing, the ancient, nameless lure lie deep within a Sussex man - too deep for time to cure! Vera Arlett

The Mid Sussex District Council sign reads: 'Most of the oak trees within Blunts Wood are English Oaks providing habitat for more than 280 species of insect, food for birds and other predators. Cavities in the trees are used by nesting birds and bats. Oaks have been held in high regard in most European cultures for centuries and were linked to Gods of thunder and lightning. Oak trees are taller than many other trees so are frequently hit by lightning'.

From Orchards car park head north to Church Road, cross and follow the footpath next to the carpark, into Trevelyan Place. At Heath Road, cross and follow the footpath descending through the ancient heath to the Cricket Pavilion, exiting at the top onto Perrymount Road. Turn right, crossing Sydney Road at the roundabout then cross left towards the Burrell Arms continuing left in front of the pub and garage towards the railway bridge. The Burrell Arms (1871) reproduced on the pub wall are those of Cuckfield landowners based at Ockenden Manor and are seen also in Cuckfield Church Lady Chapel. Immediately after the railway bridge, look right at the inclined track beyond the metal gate used years back for animals to ascend from market to the cattle trains. Cross in front of Sainsbury's heading along Bannister Way, Harlands Road, Bluntswood Road and Crescent to enter Blunts Wood at the car park continuing in the same direction. You exit onto Hatchgate Lane where you can catch a 39, 89 or 271 bus back to town opposite The Wheatsheaf pub.

2 mile/3.1km

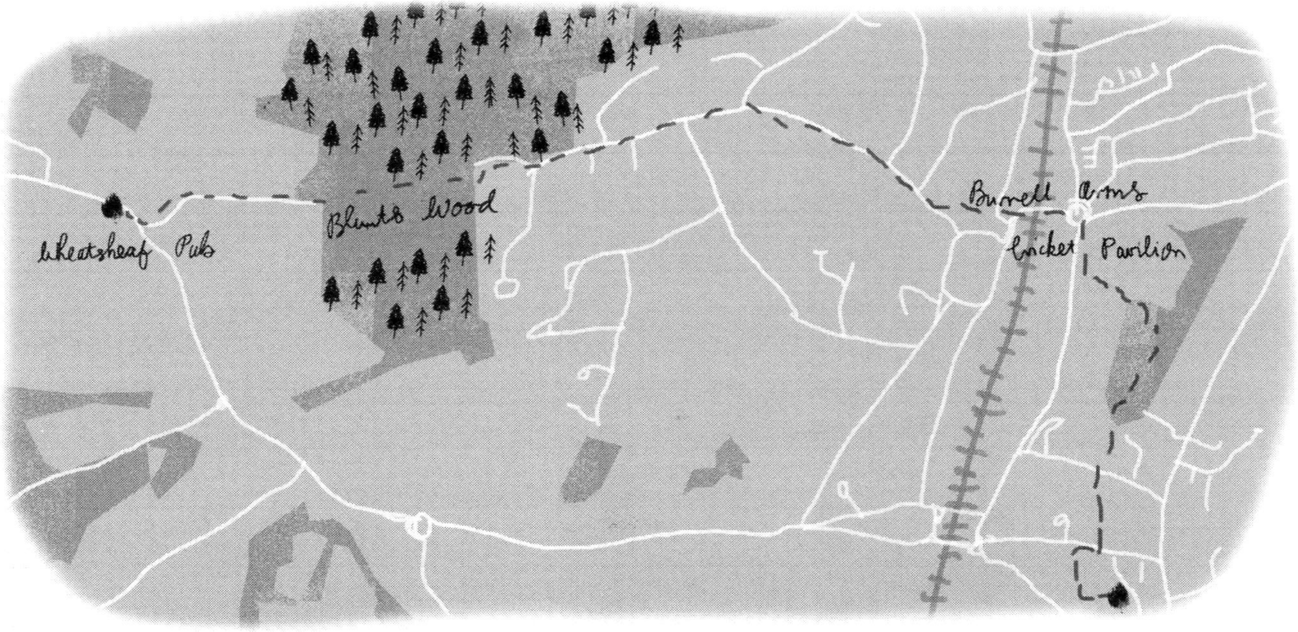

Wheatsheaf Pub
Blunts Wood
Burrell Arms
Cricket Pavilion

14   Beech Hurst

> 2 mile circular walk to Beech Hurst by way of Lucastes Road returning past Muster Green

God gives all men all earth to love, but, since man's heart is small, ordains for each one spot shall prove beloved over all. Each to his choice, and I rejoice the lot has fallen to me in a fair ground - in a fair ground - yea, Sussex by the sea! Kipling

The beautiful Lucastes Road running down from Beech Hurst (see Walk 1.1) is built on the ancient Roman Road. Lucastes prides itself in being the only road of that name in the UK with house prices in 2020 averaging a million pounds. Haywards Heath house prices are highest near the station, here easily accessed on the footpath via the Dolphin. The prices demonstrate the town's prosperity built from high paid work in London or worldwide through easy access to Gatwick Airport. Though a commuter town with little local employment for over 30,000 inhabitants (2011 census) Haywards Heath celebrates a rich history allied to that of Sussex and beautiful surrounds accessed at little cost.

From Orchards car park head north to Church Road, cross and follow the footpath next to the car park, into Trevelyan Place. At Heath Road, cross and follow the footpath descending through the heath past the Pavilion and onto Perrymount Road. Turn right, crossing before the roundabout then walking past Haywards Heath Station under the railway bridge continuing past the station back entrance. Cross right at the traffic island before the Boltro Road sign, continue along and cross onto the island with the Cuckfield sign on it. Cross again to the top of Milton Road to follow the signed footpath which passes behind the Dolphin Leisure Centre. Continue and keep to the left exiting onto Lucastes Avenue. Turn left and then first right, as indicated by the footpath sign, onto Lucastes Road. At the top of the road, turn into Knight Close and follow the hedged footpath leading up to the main road across from Beech Hurst. After visiting the grounds and its railway return to the road and turn right on the pavement of Muster Green South crossing the top of Bolnore Road. Continue along South Road passing Victoria Park on your right to Orchards.

2.2 mile/3.6 km

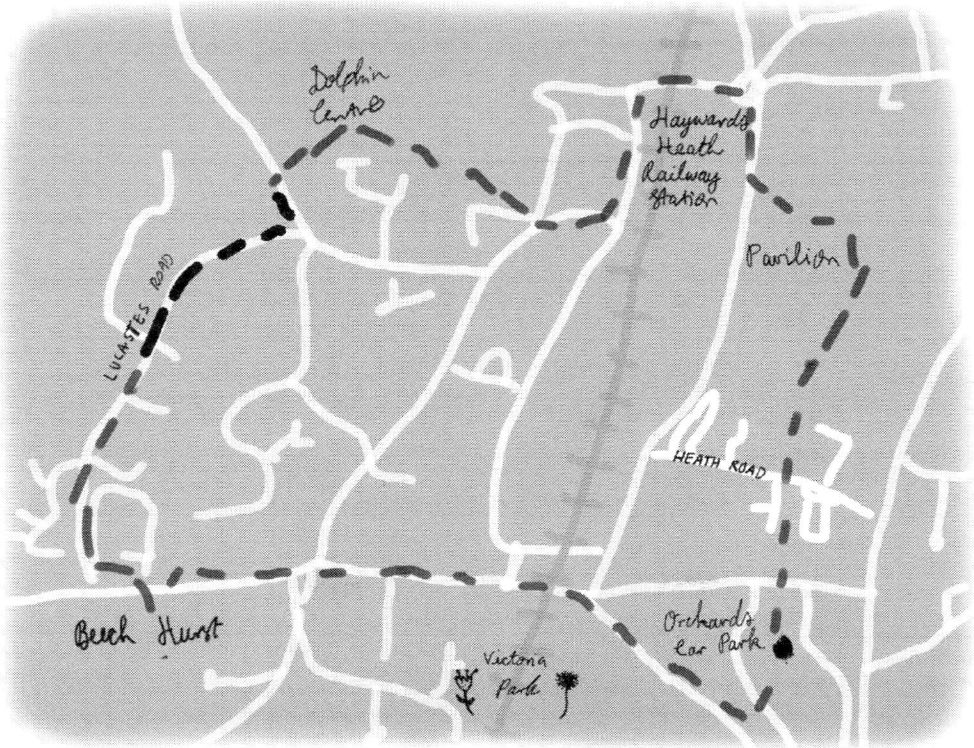
Dolphin Centre
Haywards Heath Railway Station
Pavilion
LUCASTES ROAD
HEATH ROAD
Beech Hurst
Orchards Car Park
Victoria Park

15 Donald Campbell plaque

> 3 mile walk to Lindfield via the plaques commemorating Norris House where Bluebird hydroplane was designed for Donald Campbell, and the ancient Sunte House

A journalist asked 'Are you ever afraid, Donald?' to which he replied 'Of course I'm afraid every time I get into the Bluebird. Courage is not being fearless. Courage is overcoming and smashing through fear.'
Donald Campbell

Lew and Ken Norris and Donald Campbell have a plaque in Burrell Road outside the former Norris House. This commemorates the brothers' pioneering work on jet engines including *Bluebell K7* and Donald Campbell who attempted to break the water speed record in this hydroplane with fatal consequence 4 January 1967 on Coniston Water in the Lake District. Older residents recall letters apologising for jet noise as Bluebird was tested 1966 in Burrell Road.

From Orchards car park head north to Church Road, cross and follow the footpath next to the carpark, into Trevelyan Place. At Heath Road, cross into Clair Park and follow the footpath descending through the old heath to Perrymount Road. Cross in front of Sainsbury's heading along Bannister Way and take a first right down Burrell Road to Flowserve. The Norris Brothers and Donald Campbell blue plaque is affixed to an entrance pillar. Continue walking along Burrell Road which curves left. At the junction turn left on the pavement besides Balcombe Road then first right along Old Wickham Way. Cross the railway bridge and walk on past Wickham Farmhouse, a site dating back to the 13th century. Go straight ahead into a narrow footpath that passes in front of Sunte House occupation of which can be traced back to 1522. The footpath emerges at a mini roundabout where you continue straight ahead on Sunte Avenue to the Witch Pub. Turn right then first left down Denman's Lane to the bus stop on Lindfield High Street for your return by 30, 270 or 272 bus to Orchards.

2.7 mile/4.3 km

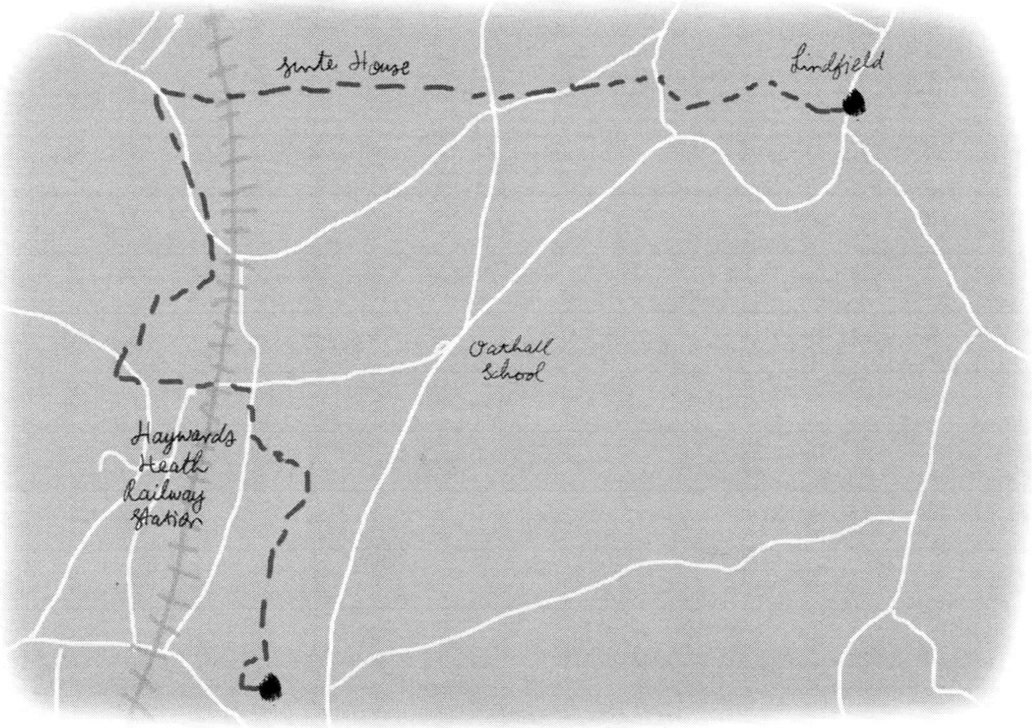

Sunte House
Lindfield
Oathall
School
Haywards
Heath
Railway
Station

World's End

> 3 mile walk through woods and fields to World's End returning by bus, possible by walking carefully away from peak traffic down a high risk section of bendy road without a verge, with alternative being dropped off at the farm track off Rocky Lane

It is not what you are or have been that God looks at with his merciful eyes, but what you would be. The Cloud of Unknowing

North east Burgess Hill is known as World's End. On 23 December 1899 when a red signal was obscured by fog the Brighton train collided at the rail junction with the boat train from Newhaven killing six passengers. Seen as a terrible thing the area became known as World's End.

From Orchards car park descend the precinct and turn right along the pavement to the pedestrian crossing. Cross and turn right along the pavement then left to enter Victoria Park. Walk diagonally across to exit the bottom south west corner into Drummond Close. Walk along the Close then turn right proceeding down Sunnywood Drive to the first junction. Turn right into Keymer End and cross the railway bridge then turn left and walk on the path nearest to the railway through Pierce's Wood. Walk up the side of the railway bridge onto Old Rocky Lane and turn left across the bridge continuing onto Rocky Lane. Turn right to walk on the pavement over the road bridge. Cross the road before the roundabout and cross again to walk with care facing traffic along Rocky Lane taking the first right towards Brooklands Farm. Alternatively arrange a lift to this point. Continue on the lane then at the T turn left onto the track away from the farm. At the next T turn right. Take the footpath on the left and walk under the pylons down to Valebridge Lake. Continue taking a right turn at the first T and left at the second to pass under the railway bridge into Valebridge Close leading to Valebridge Road, World's End. Catch a 271 or 272 bus back to Orchards.

3 mile/4.9 km

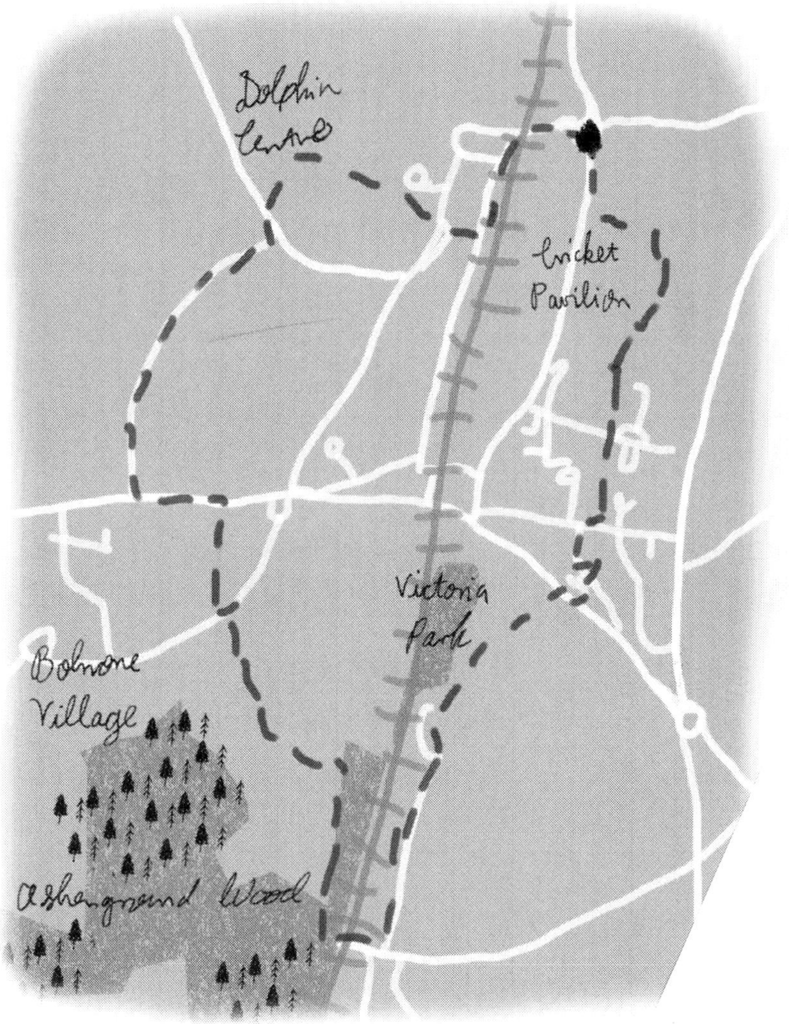

Dolphin Centre
Cricket Pavilion
Victoria Park
Bolmore Village
Ashengrund Wood

18 William Allen House

> 3 mile circular walk visiting sites associated with Quaker philanthropist William Allen whose legacy is celebrated in Haywards Heath America Estate

In the multitude of things which harness the mind, the main object is the good of others. William Allen

Haywards Heath owes an immense debt to the heart for social renewal possessed by William Allen (1770-1843) who founded the town's America estate. Allen was a man of many parts, a scientist and pharmacist, educationalist and prison reformer, pacifist and slavery abolitionist. He established a 'home colony' to build self-sufficiency and empower agricultural workers from Lindfield off Gravelye Lane. This was when people recalled the poor being sent across the Atlantic to what had then just become Britain's former colony. Haywards Heath street names recall Allen's contribution through the America estate.

From Orchards car park descend through the precinct and turn left along South Road. Continue down to the roundabout and turn left down Caxton Way continuing straight ahead down the Syresham Gardens footpath beside the stream to St Augustine's Way. Turn right then left along Priory Way to Western Road. Turn left and after North Road, cross the road to descend the footpath on the left of the Cemetery gates. Continue straight ahead at the bottom to the right of the stream into The Hollow. Continue and ascend the track at the top of the road beside No 2 which passes the grounds of William Allen House noting the brick mounting block outside Gravelye Cottage on the other side. At the top of the track turn left and left again into Gravelye Close where William Allen's former residence aka Gravelye House can be viewed on the left. Continue down Gravelye Road and take the second left down William Allen Lane. Enter Scrase Valley Reserve at the bottom continuing with the stream to your right. Turn left at the junction walking up to the recreation ground following Barn Cottage Lane then right up New England Road exiting America Estate at Hazelgrove Road. Cross to Church Road and Orchards.

3.1 mile/5 km

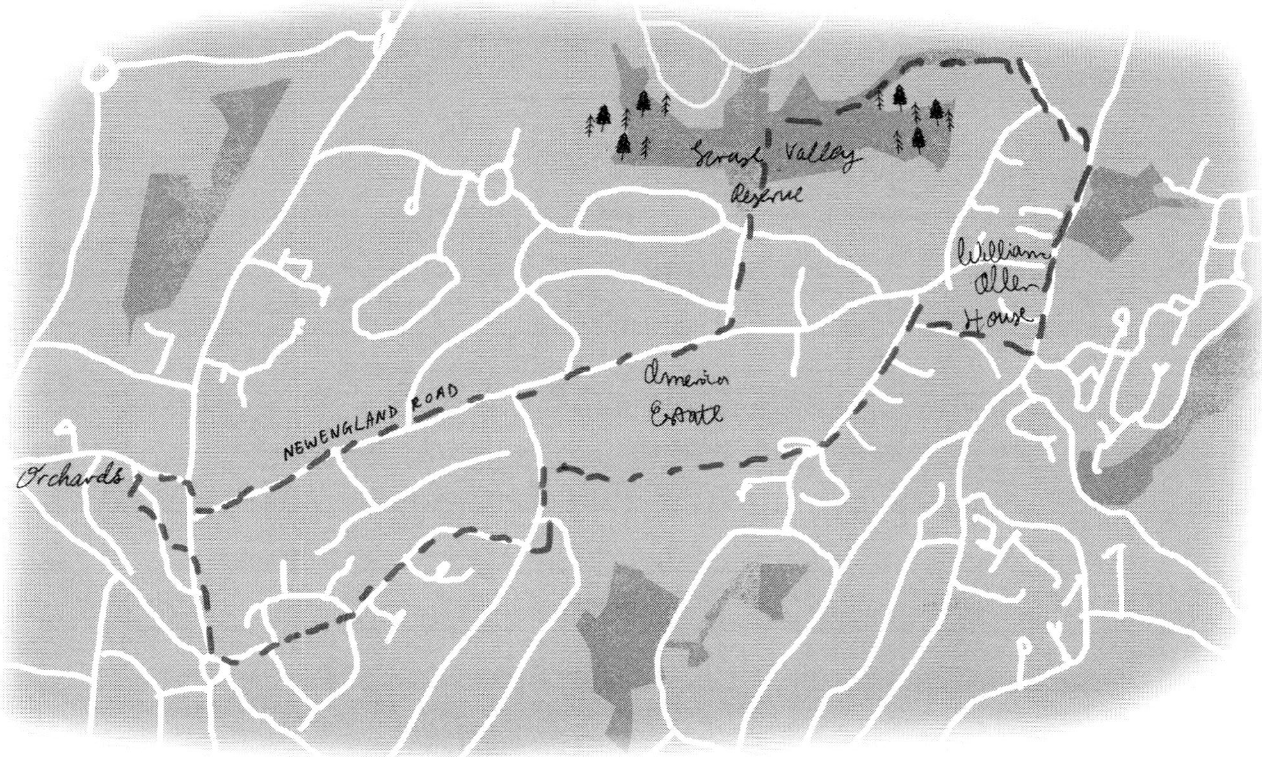

Valley
Reserve
William
Allen
House
Amenia
Estate
NEWENGLAND ROAD
Orchards

19   Cuckfield

> 3 mile walk to Cuckfield village from which Haywards Heath expanded after the arrival of the railway, returning by bus

A daughter will outgrow your lap but she will never outgrow your heart.
Anon

Cuckfield with Lindfield are parents to Haywards Heath. Their disagreement about hosting the London-Brighton railway brought the new town to birth after 1840. Prior to then they benefited as staging posts for travellers. In 1820 50 stagecoaches a day passed through Cuckfield in ancient lore 'open land inhabited by cuckoos'. Its current rural ambience contrasts with former prominence in the Elizabethan iron industry, hence place names like Furnace Wood and Cinder Banks. Holy Trinity Church is mother to St Wilfrid, Haywards Heath and has memorials to the Warden Sergison and Burrell families whose patronage of Haywards Heath is recalled in use of their names for pubs and schools.

From Orchards car park head north to Church Road, cross and follow the footpath next to the carpark, into Trevelyan Place. At Heath Road, cross and follow the footpath down the heath onto Perrymount Road. Turn right, crossing before the roundabout then walking past the Station under the bridge continuing left. Cross right at the traffic island before the Boltro Road sign, continue along and cross onto the island with the Cuckfield sign on it. Cross again to the top of Milton Road to follow the signed footpath behind the Leisure Centre exiting onto Lucastes Avenue. Turn left and then first right, as indicated by the footpath sign, onto Lucastes Road. At the top of the road, turn into Knight Close and follow the hedged footpath leading up to the main road. Turn right. After the roundabout, cross the road and take a left turn down Copyhold Lane following the public bridle way sign. You take the footpath on the right after The Limes. Cross the road and ascend the footpath turning left at the T along the wooded path behind Warden Park School. The path continues along a field providing a splendid view of the South Downs. Continue past the pond to Holy Trinity cemetery. Cuckfield Park lies beyond and Ockenden Manor, built by iron master Henry Bowyer in the 1570s. Older villagers recall the replacement of the Church spire destroyed by fire in 1980. After viewing the Church, linked to Lewes Priory in the 11th century, and its fine Kempe ceiling, proceed to the main street which retains a medieval feel. Cuckfield Museum (1981) in Queen's Hall, manned by volunteers, is a resource for both Cuckfield and Haywards Heath. Catch a 39, 89 or 271 bus back to Orchards.

3.2 mile/5.1 km

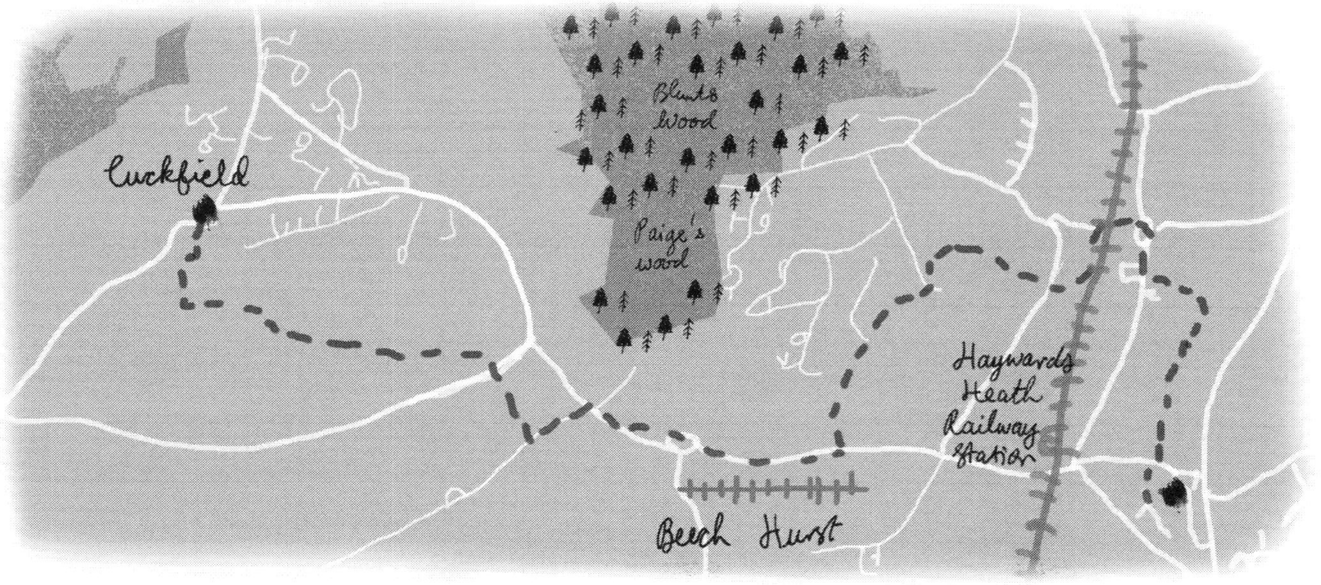
Cuckfield
Blunts Wood
Paige's wood
Beech Hurst
Haywards Heath Railway Station

20   Blunts Wood

> 3 mile circular walk past Harlands Farm to Blunts Wood returning via Lucastes Avenue

The only real test of spiritual growth is an increase of simplicity, compassion and love. Paul Harris

Blunts Wood separates Cuckfield from Haywards Heath. Though eroded by housing it remains a sizable wood with a lovely walk along its stream. Harlands means boundary and the 17th century farm of that name still standing on Bridgers Mill is on the boundary between Cuckfield and Lindfield parishes. The railway was placed on that boundary minimising impact on either village. Before the housing London railway passengers could look down on cows being gathered for milking at Harlands Farm.

Head north from Orchards car park to Church Road, cross and follow the footpath next to the carpark, into Trevelyan Place. At Heath Road, cross into Clair Park and follow the footpath descending through the old heath and left past the Cricket Pavilion to Perrymount Road. Cross in front of Sainsbury's heading along Bannister Way and take a first right down Burrell Road which curves left. Turn left down Bridgersmill to view Harlands Farmhouse after the right bend. Return to Burrell Road, turn left into Balcombe Road, left again down Barnmead and take the pathway on the left between no's 74 and 76 up to Penland Road. Cross to the right of the entrance to Harlands School and join the footpath into Blunts Wood. Stay on the path which keeps the school fence to your left. This path continues out of the wood through a new housing development back into the wood crossing the stream. Take the narrow path up on your left immediately after the bridge and continue with the stream on your left until the next bridge. Cross and make the steep ascent to Blunts Wood Road. Turn left and then first right along Lucastes Avenue continuing to the footpath sign. Follow the path to the left. Continue keeping right at the junction to walk behind the Leisure Centre up to Milton Road. Turn right then and, with care, left at the end of the railings to the traffic island. Cross again, walk down to cross Boltro Road and turn left walking past the station side entrance. Continue under the railway bridge across the main station entrance and turn right at the roundabout. Cross Perrymount Road into the car park walking diagonally up to the Cricket Pavilion then keeping right up through the heath to Heath Road. Cross the road and continue along the footpath next to the car park into Church Road and then through either St Joseph's or St Wilfrid's Way into Orchards car park.

3.2 mile/5.2 km

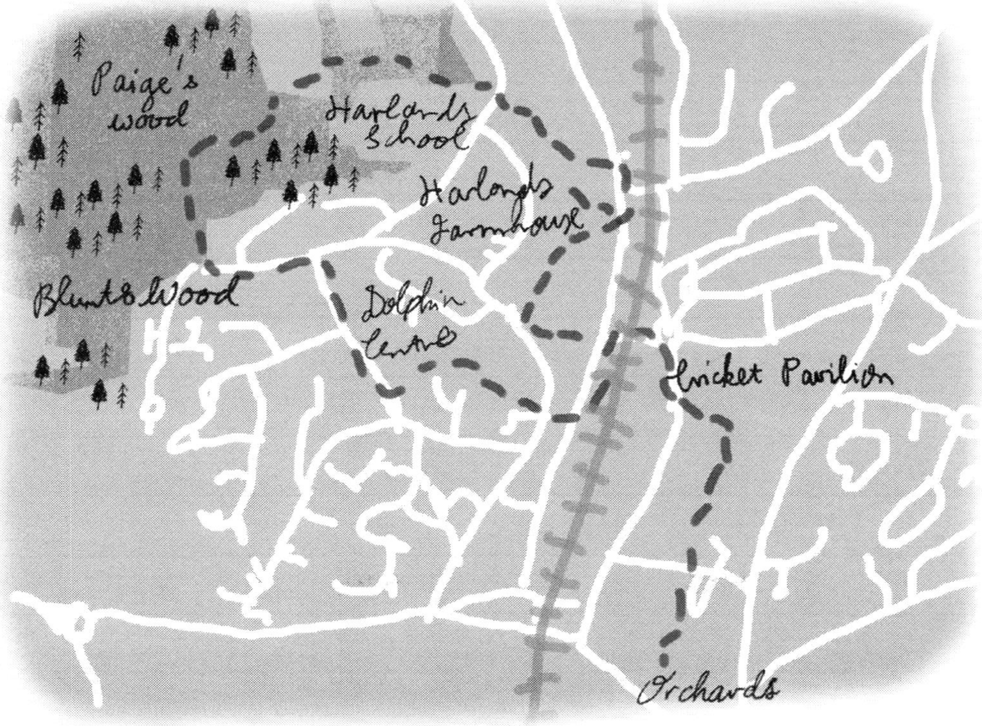
Paige's wood
Harlands School
Harlands Farmhouse
Blunts Wood
Dolphin Centre
Cricket Pavilion
Orchards

21 Scaynes Hill

> 4 mile walk to Scaynes Hill returning by bus

So many people of good will would become persons of noble soul if only they would not panic and resolve the painful tensions within their lives too prematurely. Jacques Maritain

Scaynes Hill like Haywards Heath lies on high ground which attracted early settlement on account of good drainage. The A272 running through the village continues from Winchester to Heathfield, sometimes called the pilgrim route to Canterbury, though now questioned. The dedication of Scaynes Hill Church is to St Augustine of Canterbury. Local history is symbolised on the 1977 Queen's Jubilee Village sign on Lewes Road with anchor, trowel, saw and bunch of grapes. The Farmers pub (1751) was once known as 'The Anchor' from a holding place at the top of the hill helping haul loads up the steep road. The trowel and saw signify the now defunct village builders and saw mill and the grapes Rock Lodge vineyard. Scaynes Hill quarry provided the orange sandstone for Lancing College dedicated 1911.

From Orchards car park descend through the precinct and turn left along South Road. Continue down to the roundabout and turn left down Caxton Way continuing straight ahead down the Syresham Gardens footpath beside the stream to St Augustine's Way. Turn right then left along Priory Way to Western Road. Turn left and cross the road into the footpath down to the left of the Cemetery gates. Continue left at the bottom of the graveyard then right into Silver Birches, left into The Hollow and walk on to No. 2. Go up the track to Gravelye Lane and cross diagonally in effect to enter Lyoth Lane. Continue up the steep narrow road to Snowdrop Lane and turn left walking past Snowdrop Inn on a beautiful country lane to its junction with the B2111 Lewes Road. Cross diagonally following the footpath sign through into a narrow path along a field. At the end enter a farm track continuing to a . After the enter a large field and cross straight ahead to enter the wood. Follow the footpath through the woods, which eventually runs parallel to overhead cables, up to Church Road, Scaynes Hill. Turn right and walk along the road which has on the right a Strict Baptist Church and then St Augustine's Parish Church. The latter is often open and contains a large tapestry woven by villagers 1991-9 featuring Christ as represented in St John's Gospel. Continue to the petrol station and cross Lewes Road to catch the 31 Uckfield bus back to Orchards.

3.7 mile/5.9 km

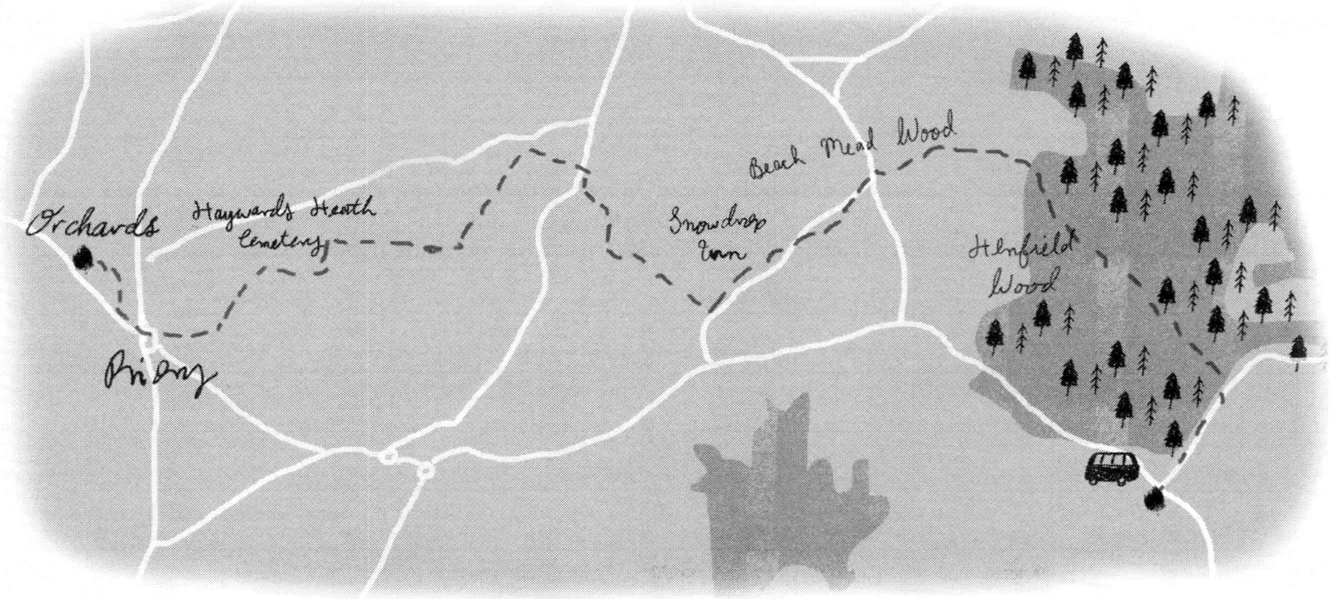
Orchards
Haywards Heath Cemetery
Priory
Snowdrop Inn
Beach Mead Wood
Henfield Wood

Wivelsfield Church

> 4 mile walk to Wivelsfield Church returning by bus

Unhappiness is the refusal to suffer. George Scott-Moncrieff

Lunces Hall at the end of Church Lane in Wivelsfield belonged to a family with lands among the most extensive in Sussex so that Burgess Hill was built on lands from the west of the estate. Wifel, whose field this village was, may have been first owner of the Hall given an 8th-century reference to the village as Wifelesfeld. Grade II listed St Peter & St John the Baptist Church is 11th century with Saxon door and north aisle added 19th century. The splendid Yew Tree in the churchyard is older than the building.

From Orchards head east across the car park, then right down St Joseph's Way to Hazelgrove Road. Continue down to the roundabout and turn left down Caxton Way continuing straight ahead down the Syresham Gardens footpath beside the stream to St Augustine's Way. Turn right then left along Priory Way to Western Road. Turn left and cross the road into the footpath down to the left of the Cemetery gates. Turn left and cross the road into the Cemetery. Walk down to the bottom, turn right and exit onto a path through the wood, and at the footpath junction turn left to ascend the tarmac slope. Cross the road taking the footpath ahead to enter Franklands Village recreation ground. Turn right when you reach Gravelye Lane, heading past the village shop onto Northlands Avenue. Cross the Avenue and continue up to the petrol station and the path which follows behind it to Birch Hotel built by Harley Street Doctor Jowers linked with the old hospital. From the Hotel cross Lewes Road into the footpath along Hurstwood Lane. Descend to the Fox & Hounds Pub keeping alert for traffic. Cross Lunces Hill, named after Wivelsfield's patrons, and walk left from the pub to the Haywards Heath sign. Leave the road at the sign heading half right onto the concrete track to Griggs Farmhouse. Continue on the track beside the hedge under pylon-held cables to a metal gate. Follow the footpath beyond with the hedge to your left which steers left to a path junction. Take a left turn up the steps and over the then along to a kissing gate by Lunces Hall. Continue left along Church Lane to Wivelsfield Church. After your visit head to the bus stop at the top of Church Lane returning by 149, 166, 271 or 272 bus to Haywards Heath.

3.7 mile/6 km

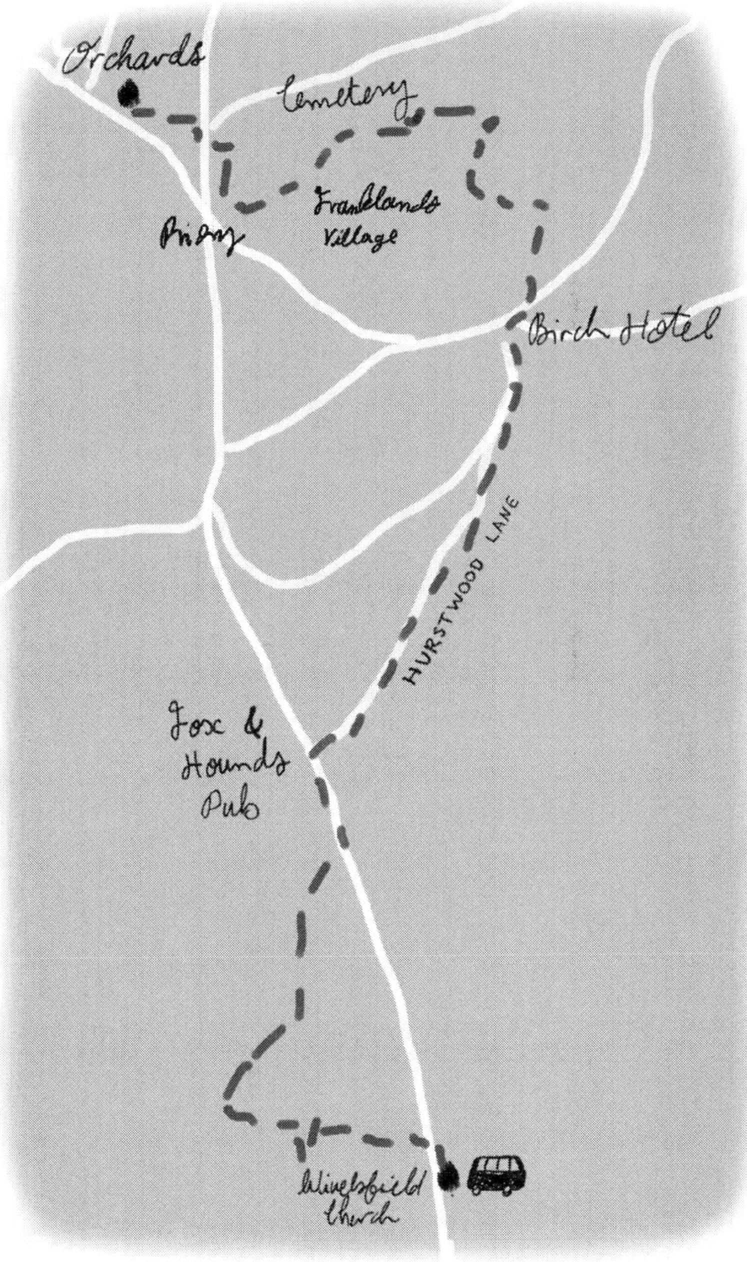
Orchards
Cemetery
Franklands
Village
Priory
Birch Hotel
HURSTWOOD LANE
Fox &
Hounds
Pub
Wivelsfield
Church

23   Ansty

> 4 mile walk to Ansty hamlet returning by bus

Love, however lashed, is not driven out. The more it is defenceless, the more it shows itself almighty. Austin Farrer

Sussex place names can be tricky to pronounce. When people mention them they betray their familiarity or unfamiliarity with the locality. Ansty like Ardingly is pronounced with heavy stress on the last syllable i.e. An-stye. Haywards Heath commuters are most familiar with Ansty as the fastest way in and out of the town from the A23 London to Brighton Road. This walk across the fields from Haywards Heath is a discovery of the hamlet for itself beyond its significance on the fast road out of town. There is a petrol service station for refreshments before catching the Horsham bus back to Haywards Heath or walking into Cuckfield for a more frequent bus to Orchards.

Head north from Orchards car park to Church Road, cross and follow the footpath next to the carpark, into Trevelyan Place. At Heath Road, cross and follow the footpath descending through the heath past the Pavilion onto Perrymount Road. Turn right, crossing before the roundabout then walking past Haywards Heath Station under the railway bridge continuing past the station back entrance. Cross right at the traffic island before the Boltro Road sign, continue along and cross onto the island with the Cuckfield sign on it. Cross again to the top of Milton Road to follow the signed footpath which passes behind the Dolphin Leisure Centre. Continue and keep to the left exiting onto Lucastes Avenue. Turn left and then first right, as indicated by the footpath sign, onto Lucastes Road. At the top of the road, turn into Knight Close and follow the hedged footpath leading up to the main road. Turn right. You pass in front of two historic buildings mainly concealed by hedges mentioned on the 1638 Hayworth map. Steeple Cottage is named there as the then Court House. Butler's Green House was home from the 17th century of the Warden family whose name has been applied to the local Warden Park schools. After the roundabout, cross the road and take a left turn down Copyhold Lane following the public bridle way sign past Lodge Farm. Take a right turn at Copyhold Cottage then continue left as a path joins from your right. Go through a gate and follow the path down to a bridge over the stream. Ascend the steps after this, turning left onto a gravelled track. Follow this track to Birch Trees Farm and the A272. Catch the 89 bus back to Orchards.

3.9 mile/6.2 km

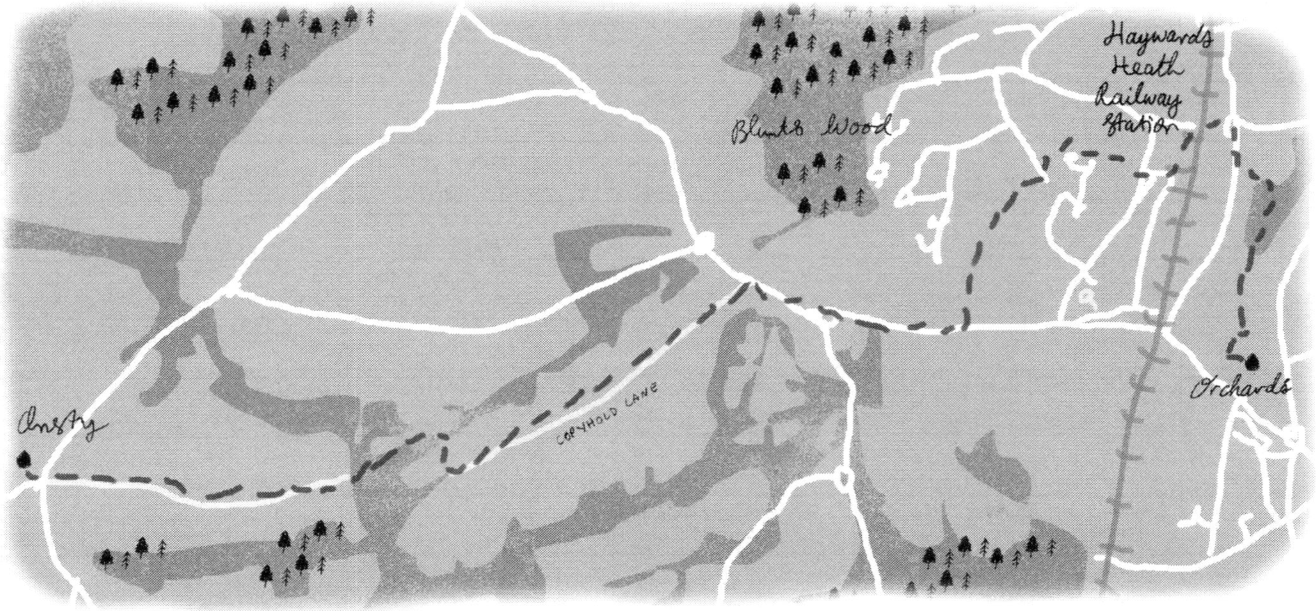
Haywards
Heath
Railway
Station
Blunts Wood
Orchards
COPYHOLD LANE
Ansty

Slugwash Lane

> The South Downs provide a grand sight on this 5 mile walk to Wivelsfield Green along Slugwash Lane returning by bus

The men that live in the South Country are the kindest and most wise, they get their laughter from the loud surf, and the faith in their happy eyes comes surely from our Sister the Spring, when over the sea she flies; the violets suddenly bloom at her feet, she blesses us with surprise.
Hilaire Belloc

As the M25 skirts the North Downs south of London and the A27 skirts the South Downs and Brighton the A272 traverses the ancient home of Haywards Heath, the High Weald of Mid-Sussex. Heather Warnes 2009 history observes that 'it was common in this part of Mid Sussex for early estates to be laid out across a ridge top, the north-facing slopes often being reserved to the lord for wood and timber'. The heath was open land facing south benefitting both from the sun and drainage of water from the rock underlay of the High Weald down to the southern claylands. Wivelsfield Green east of the historic village of Wivelsfield is part of the Low Weald we descend to on this walk heading towards the South Downs visible on the horizon.

From Orchards car park descend through the precinct and turn left along South Road. Continue down to the roundabout and turn left down Caxton Way continuing straight ahead down the Syresham Gardens footpath beside the stream to St Augustine's Way. Turn right then left along Priory Way to Western Road. Turn left and cross the road into the footpath down to the left of the Cemetery gates. Continue left at the bottom of the graveyard then right into Silver Birches, left into The Hollow and walk on to No. 2. Go up the track to Gravelye Lane and cross diagonally in effect to enter Lyoth Lane. Continue up the steep narrow road to Snowdrop Lane, turn right and walk to Lewes Road. Cross the road with care. Turn left to walk along the path and verge turning right after a distance into Slugwash Lane. After Slugwash Kennels & Cattery follow the bends in the road. At the top of the hill after the two safety mirrors opposite Townings Place before the White House turn right onto the footpath through the wooden gate and proceed along a fence then hedge on your right then heading half left to a gate. Head across the large field to the right of the water tank towards the gate in the gap in the trees. Proceed along the concrete track beyond the gate crossing the on your left then walking across the field to the main road. Cross the B2112 to catch the 166, 271 or 272 bus back to Orchards.

4.7 mile/7.5 km

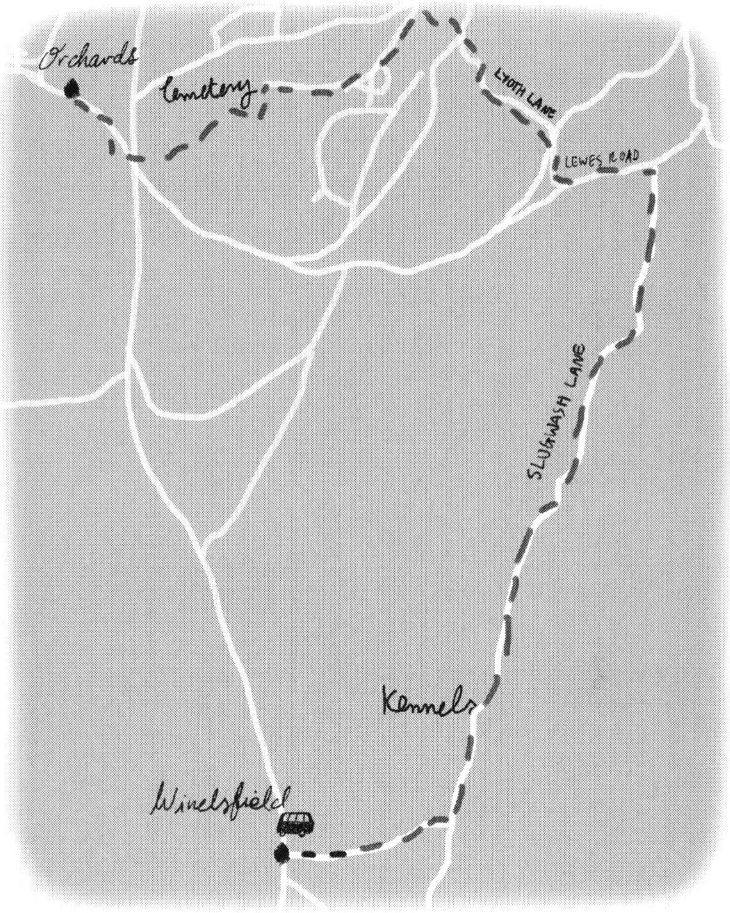

Orchards
Cemetery
LYOTH LANE
LEWES ROAD
SLUGWASH LANE
Kennels
Wivelsfield

25   Abbots Leigh

> 5 mile circular walk crossing Lewes Road taking in a view of Abbots Leigh house

In the hands of God mud is as transparent as light. De Caussade

Abbots Leigh House (1892) built by an aide of Queen Victoria recalls a village near Bristol and a hymn tune composed there in 1942 by villager Cyril Taylor for 'Glorious things of thee are spoken' to replace use of the German national anthem. It is a hidden treasure of Haywards Heath with a facade visible only from the footpath which circles the estate.

From Orchards car park go down through the precinct and turn left along South Road. Continue down to the roundabout and turn left down Caxton Way continuing straight ahead down the Syresham Gardens footpath beside the stream to St Augustine's Way. Turn right then left along Priory Way to Western Road. Turn left and cross the road into the footpath down to the left of the Cemetery gates. Continue left at the bottom of the graveyard then right into Silver Birches, left into The Hollow and walk on to No. 2. Go up the track to Gravelye Lane and cross diagonally in effect to enter Lyoth Lane. After Bramble Lodge and Outwood ascend the footpath on your right alongside the rustic fence. At the top cross The Oaks between two tall hedges into the continuing path. Cross Cobbetts Mead into the last section of this ancient path slippery in rain. Cross Lewes Road and go down the footpath to the right of North Colwell Barn. The woodland path opens into a large well mown meadow. Follow the path down through the fields as it curves round Abbots Leigh revealed in all its splendour to viewers on the path in the bottom field. After enjoying the view enter the wood and continue through to enter Slugwash Lane opposite Cottage of Content. Turn left to walk up Slugwash Lane to Lewes Road. Turn left to walk along the verge and path before carefully crossing the road into Snowdrop Lane. Take the left turn signed for Lyoth Lane. At the bottom of the lane cross Gravelye Lane to pass down the track diagonally opposite into America Lane. Walk up New England Road crossing Hazelgrove Road into Church Road and Orchards car park.

5.3 mile/8.5 km

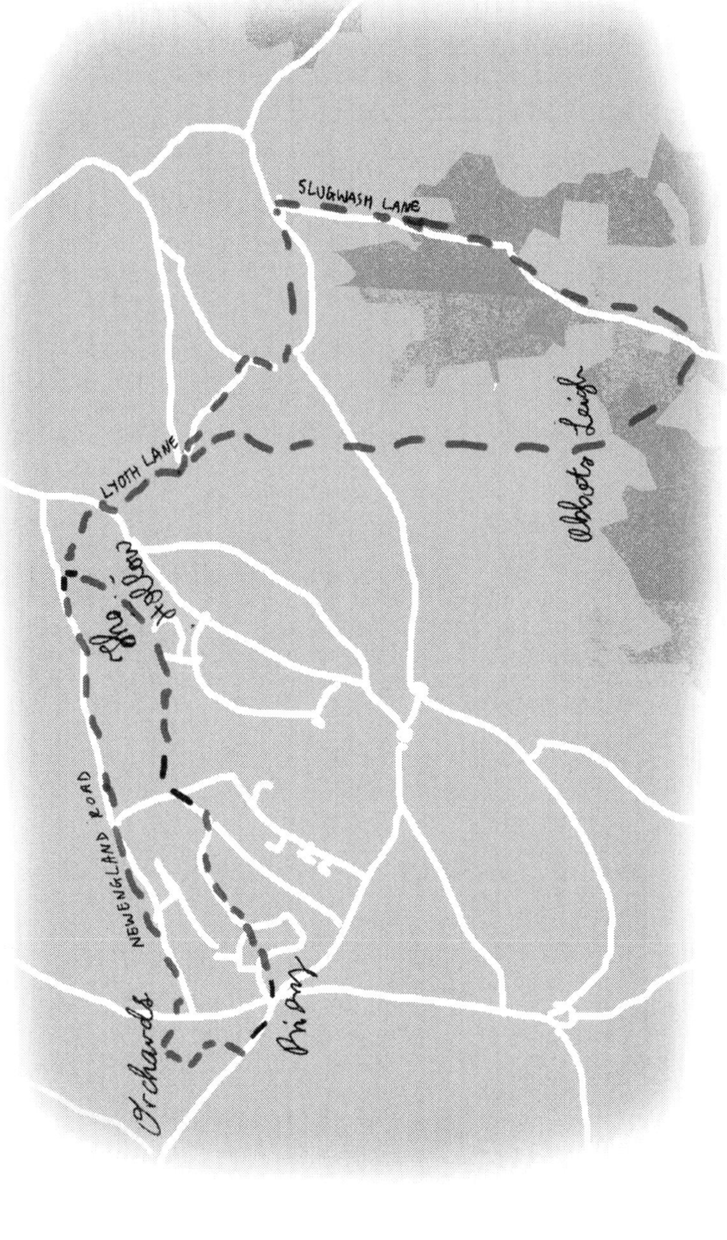
SLUGWASH LANE
LYOTH LANE
NEWENGLAND ROAD
Abbots Leigh
Orchards
Priory

Horsted Keynes

> 5 mile walk via Lindfield and East Mascalls crossing Bluebell Railway to Tremaines and Horsted Keynes returning by bus

Jaw-jaw is better than war-war. Harold Macmillan

The village of Horsted Keynes is famous for its Grade I Norman Church of lavish proportions, the volunteer-run Bluebell Railway and its association with former Prime Minister Harold Macmillan (1894-1986) buried in the Churchyard. President Kennedy visited Macmillan in the village. Margaret Thatcher attended his funeral. Less well known are two 17th century writers. Archbishop Robert Leighton (1611-1684) whose altar tomb lies outside the south wall near the side door is a saint in the Anglican calendar famed for biblical commentaries and large hearted spiritual vision. Rector Giles Moore's tomb (d1679) is less evident but his writings are also read today. 'Giles Moore's Day Book' is available on the internet providing a day-by-day record of the life of a country priest through receipts, payments and journeys in Horsted Keynes 1656-1679.

From Orchards car park head up to Church Road and turn right. Cross Hazelgrove Road and turn right heading left down New England Road. After the shops turn left along Barn Cottage Lane with the recreation ground to your right. Cross Hanbury Lane and continue down the path between the houses into Scrase Valley Reserve. After 200 yards turn right at the junction and follow the Scrase stream on your left. Exit the Reserve into Croxton Lane keeping the stream to your left and cross the bridge on the advertised public footpath into Meadow Drive. Cross the Drive to continue on the footpath opposite which leads into Lindfield Common recreation ground. Walk across the field aiming in between the seats off Lewes Road. Cross ditch and road to enter Eastern Road turning left up Luxford Road and then Barncroft Drive. As the Drive veers right turn left into the footpath. Continue straight ahead with a large field on your left until the T at a fence. Turn right and continue in the same direction ignoring the right turn crossing two s before walking along the River Ouse on your left to the road. Turn left walking past East Mascalls Farm and the Paxhill Park Golf Course to the wood. Leave the road ascending the path to your right leading into a large field. Cross the field back to the road along which the path continues briefly to Cockhaise Farm. Turn left here along a track. Take a half right turn along a footpath which descends to cross Bluebell Railway and then skirts below Tremaines Manor to the road. Turn left and walk into Horsted Keynes. Take the 270 bus back to Orchards.

5.4 mile/8.6 km

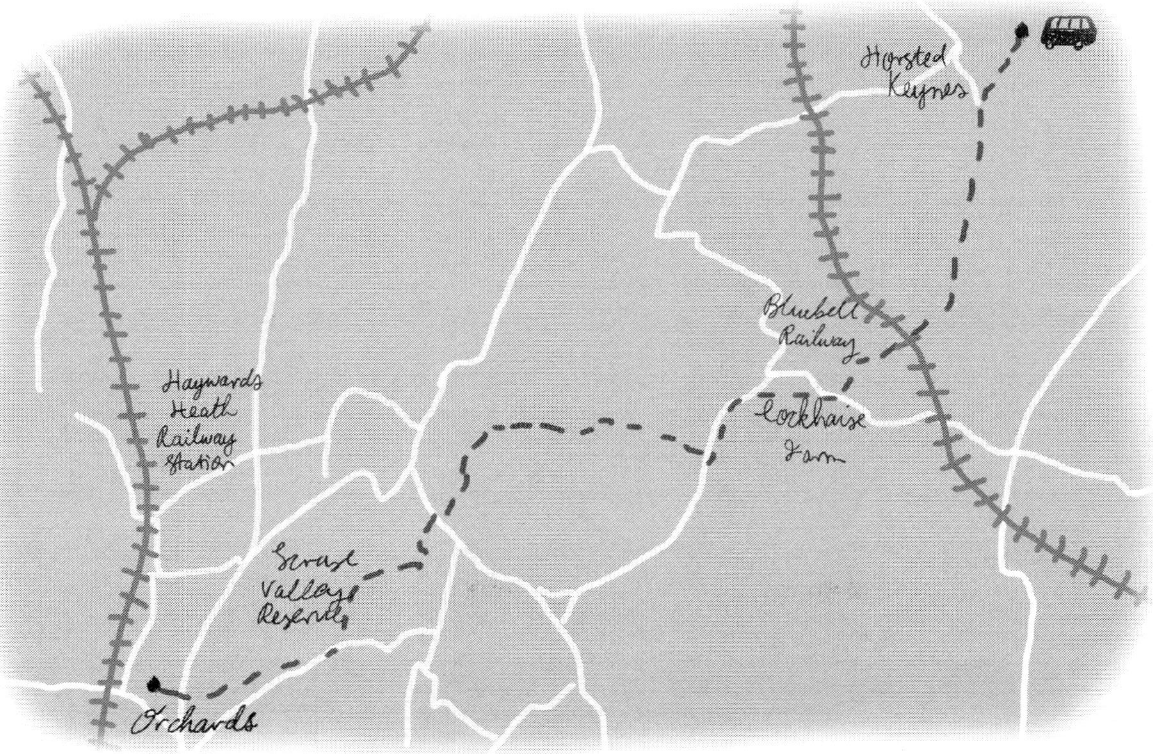
Horsted Keynes
Bluebell Railway
Cockhaise Farm
Haywards Heath Railway Station
Scrase Valley Reserve
Orchards

27   Ardingly High Weald

> 5 mile walk through Lindfield and Hill House Farm along the High Weald trail to Ardingly returning by bus

We are all in the gutter, but some of us are looking at the stars.
Oscar Wilde

Ardingly is circled by the High Weald Landscape Trail on its 90 mile journey from Horsham to the eastern extremity of Sussex at Rye taking in sights of outstanding beauty. The Trail arrives in Ardingly from Cuckfield on its way to West Hoathly.

Head up to Church Road from Orchards car park and turn right. Cross Hazelgrove Road and turn right heading left down New England Road. After the shops turn left along Barn Cottage Lane with the recreation ground to your right. Cross Hanbury Lane and continue down the path between the houses into Scrase Valley Reserve. After 200 yards turn right at the junction and follow the Scrase stream on your left. Exit the Reserve into Croxton Lane keeping the stream to your left and cross the bridge on the advertised public footpath into Meadow Drive. Cross the Drive to continue on the footpath opposite which leads into Lindfield Common recreation ground. Walk across the field aiming in between the seats off Lewes Road. Cross ditch and road to enter Eastern Road turning left up Luxford Road and then Barncroft Drive. As the Drive veers right turn left into the footpath. Continue straight ahead with a large field on your left until the T at a fence. Turn left down the path to All Saints. Turn left before the Church passing through the Churchyard to the High Street. Cross this and continue right out of the village turning left into Spring Lane. Continue respectfully through the grounds of Fulling Mill Farm through the farmyard gate to the footbridge below. Follow signs through the copse, which can be muddy, and ascend to the right of a large field to the road. Turn left at the road walking up to Hill House Farm gate and follow the footpath to the left of this. Pass through a gate before houses. The grassy track narrows to a covered footpath. Keep straight ahead at the junction continuing along the permissive footpath across a stream and up the steps of the old railway embankment. Continue right along the track then left as signed down to the left. Turn right then immediately left as signed to follow the path out of the wood. Continue on the path up the meadow. Head right then left at the top as signed continuing straight at the signpost noting a left turn to Ardingly College. Walk on over a by a gate through the fields over another and gate heading straight over a concrete track passing the standing footpath sign. Head up the field to the at the top. Continue up the next field into the hedged path to the houses where there is a seat to look back at the Downs.

Follow the metalled track to the main road. Turn left along the pavement. Cross to catch the 272 Orchards at the bus stop opposite Hapstead Hall.

5.4 mile/8.7 km

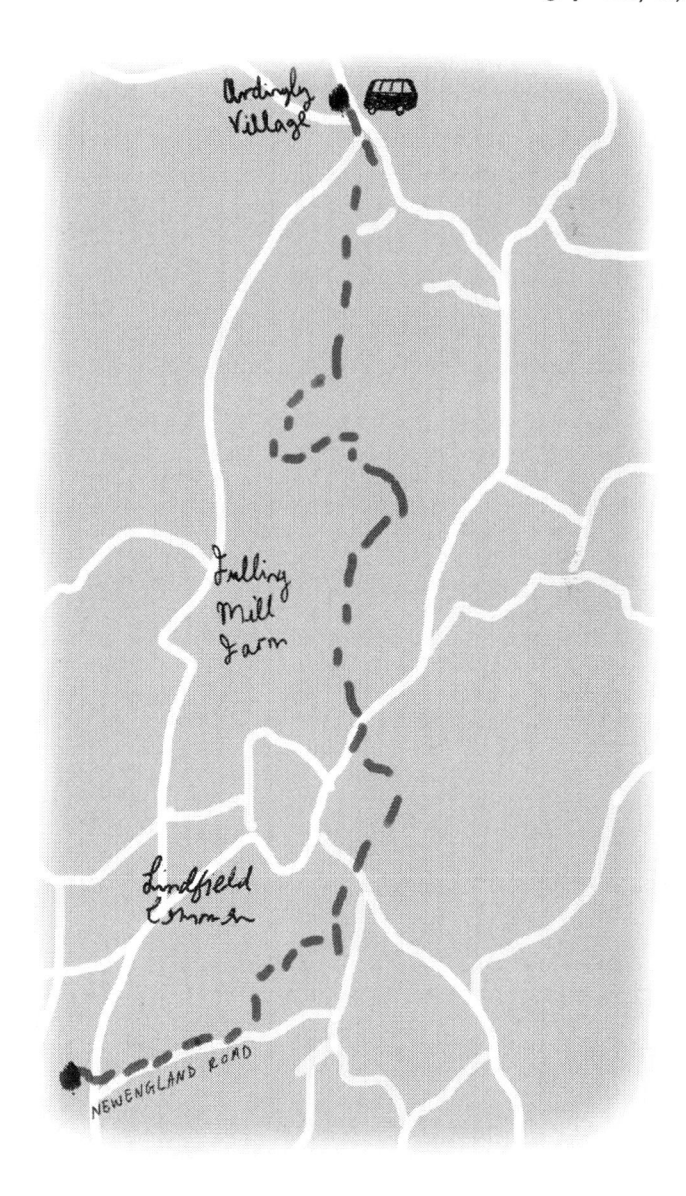

Lindfield

> 6 mile circular walk to Lindfield via Walstead

Sussex, who shall marvel if painters learn from thee new colours in the milk-soft sky, new lights on land and sea? F.W.Bourdillon

The lime trees lining the main street are true to the name 'Lindfield' meaning 'open land with lime trees'. On that street there are some forty timber-framed houses some of medieval origin leading up from the spring-fed pond with its ducks and herons at the bottom, to All Saints Church at the top. The original Church built 14th century in the Early English style was heavily restored in the 19th century. By the 1850s its churchyard was so full new burials had to be made on top of old which explains the raised ground in the northern part of the churchyard. Recognition of the health risks of this led to a decision to build a new cemetery at Walstead, a mile across the fields to the south east. The new cemetery recognised religious diversity in providing mortuary chapels for both Church of England and Nonconformist use.

From Orchards car park descend through the precinct and turn left along South Road. Continue down to the roundabout and turn left down Caxton Way continuing straight ahead down the Syresham Gardens footpath beside the stream to St Augustine's Way. Turn right then left along Priory Way to Western Road. Turn left and cross the road into the footpath down to the left of the Cemetery gates. Continue left at the bottom of the graveyard then right into Silver Birches, left into The Hollow and walk on to No. 2. Go up the track to Gravelye Lane and cross diagonally in effect to enter Lyoth Lane. Take the second turning before the stream into the housing estate and follow the footpath along Trefoil Avenue keeping the houses to your left enjoying the woods and fields to your right. Continue along the footpath and estate roads which exit onto the B2111 at Scamps Hill. Turn right and then left at the road junction walking past the cemetery. At Snowflake Lane turn left to Walstead Forge where the road narrows into a footpath. This section can be muddy after rain. Continue in the same direction to the footpath junction taking the left turn towards Lindfield. Continue straight ignoring the right turn for Lindfield village following the path between fields which enters Bancroft Drive. Head right down the Drive, cross Newton Road and proceed down Luxford Road and Eastern Road to Lewes Road. Cross into Lindfield Common recreation ground heading straight towards the tennis courts and then left into the access footpath at the field corner. Cross Meadow Drive into the next stretch of footpath passing over Scrase stream into William Allen Lane. Enter Scrase Valley Reserve continuing with the stream to your right. Turn left at the junction walking up and across to Barn Cottage Lane.

After the recreation ground, turn right up New England Road to Hazelgrove Road. Cross to Church Road and Orchards.

5.5 mile/8.9km

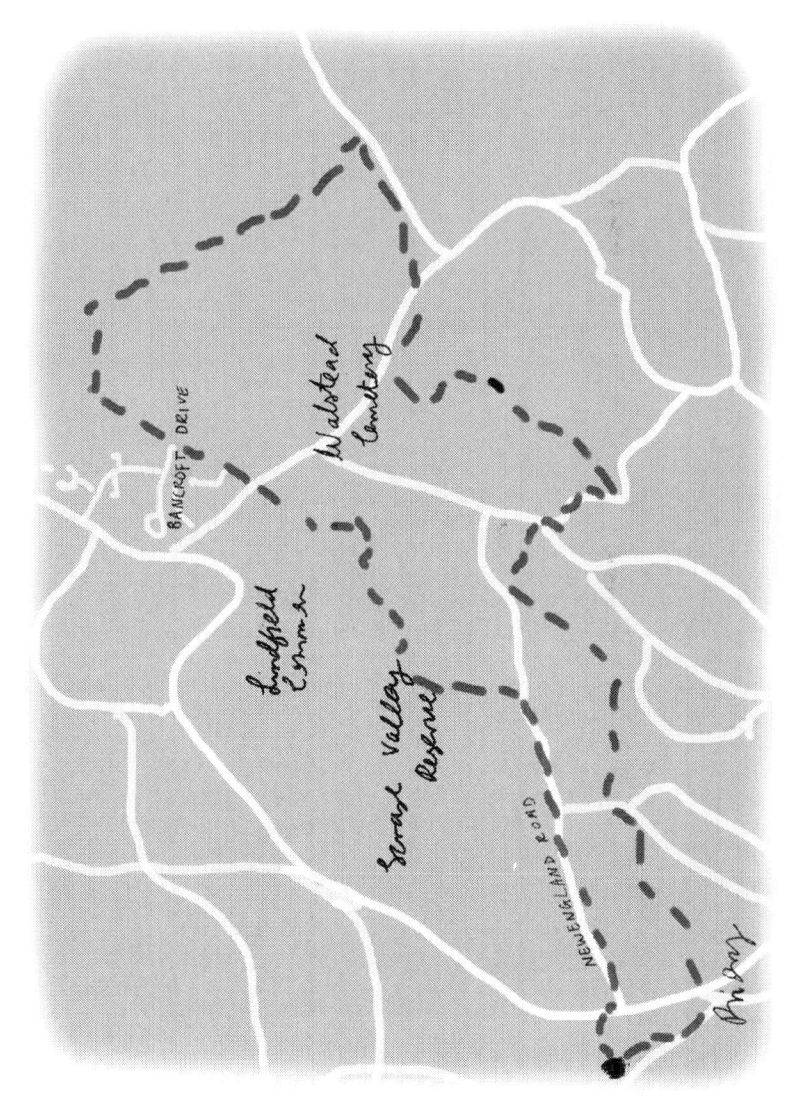

29   Kenwards Farm

> 6 mile circular walk via America Estate and Lindfield to Kenwards Farm returning via Haywards Heath Golf Course, Wickham Farm and the Railway Station

Whoever tries to dive below the calm water of his self-illusion, to humble himself and learn his true self, experiences the even stronger thrust of his own pride that tends to lift him above himself, so that he may emerge and remain on the surface. Raniero Cantalamessa

From Orchards car park go up to Church Road and turn right. Cross Hazelgrove Road and turn right heading left down New England Road. After the shops turn left along Barn Cottage Lane with the recreation ground to your right. Cross Hanbury Lane and continue down the path between the houses into Scrase Valley Local Nature Reserve. After 200 yards turn right at the junction and follow the Scrase stream on your left. At one point you duck under a large pipe. Exit the Reserve into Croxton Lane keeping the stream to your left and cross the bridge on the advertised public footpath into Meadow Drive. Cross the Drive to continue on the footpath opposite which leads to the tennis courts at the southern corner of Lindfield Common recreation ground. Continue diagonally across the field to enter Lindfield High Street. Head past All Saints Church and turn left before the right bend entering the footpath running behind the houses. This path ends on Finches Lane. Turn right and follow the track through the woods to a junction with the road into Kenwards Farm. Turn left to the main road and cross into the wood straight up the path which follows the edge of the field then zig zags through the trees. Turn right at the fork then right again at a second fork which veers left continuing on the old railway embankment near Copyhold Lane. At its end descend carefully to the footpath by the gate to the Lane but head left away from that to the Golf Course. Turn right to walk initially with the Golf Course on your left. Follow the footpath signs straight ahead. They take you into an ancient covered path which ascends to the walls of Wickham Farm. Turn right onto Old Wickham Lane and shortly left into Wickham Way descending to College Road with St Wilfrid's on the horizon. Cross College Road, turn right and immediately left up Mill Green Road ascending to the roundabout and beyond it. Head left through the car park to the Cricket Pavilion and continue right on the path through the ancient heath to Heath Road. Cross the road and continue along the footpath next to the car park into Church Road and then into Orchards car park.

5.6 mile/ 9 km

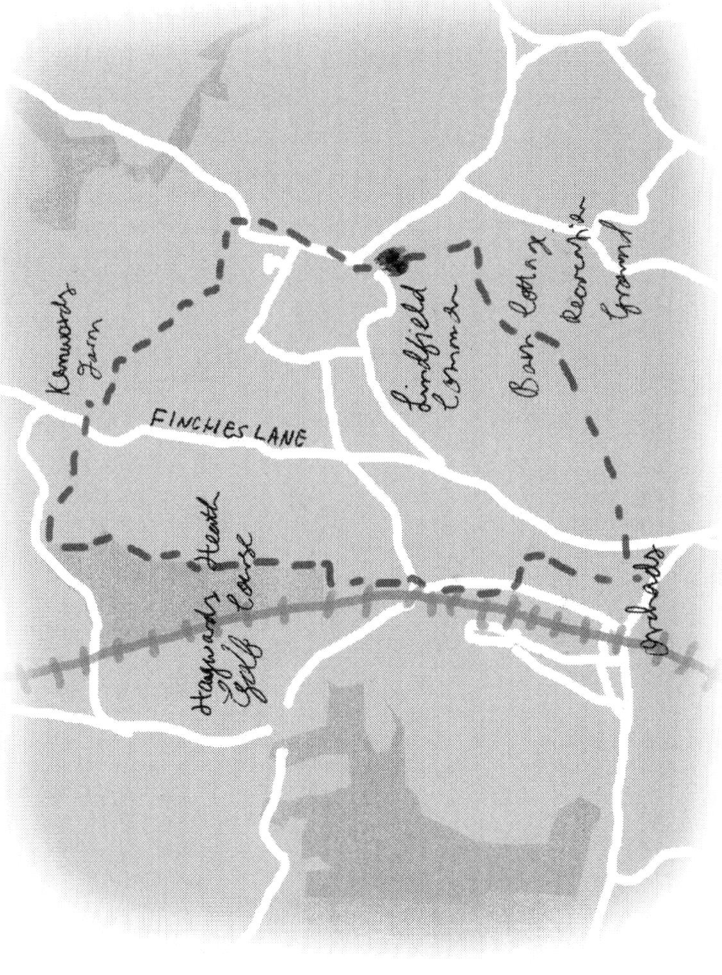

Kenwards Farm
FINCHES LANE
Lindfield Common
Barn Cottage
Recreation Ground
Haywards Heath Golf Course
Orchards

Cuckfield

> 6 mile walk via Beech Hurst to Cuckfield Church returning through Blunts Wood

Set in the key of blue, with harmonies bee-brown, is Cuckfield, land of green and dew, with hanging woods and opulent chestnut trees set in the key of blue. When Sussex' downs were leafier, and more new the wonders of the woodlands and the seas, this Lowland love was 'Field of the Cuckoo'. Then some new Poet, seeking images for towns, heard Cuckoo-calls, and christened you The Cuckoo Field, land of golden melodies set in the key of blue. Victor Neuburg

From Orchards car park head north to Church Road, cross and follow the footpath next to the carpark, into Trevelyan Place. At Heath Road, cross and follow the footpath down the heath onto Perrymount Road. Turn right, crossing before the roundabout then walking past the Station under the bridge continuing left. Cross right at the traffic island before the Boltro Road sign, continue along and cross onto the island with the Cuckfield sign on it. Cross again to the top of Milton Road to follow the signed footpath behind the Leisure Centre exiting onto Lucastes Avenue. Turn left and then first right, as indicated by the footpath sign, onto Lucastes Road. At the top of the road, turn into Knight Close and follow the hedged footpath leading up to Beech Hurst on the main road. Turn right. After the roundabout, cross the road and take a left turn down Copyhold Lane following the public bridle way sign. You take the footpath on the right after The Limes. Cross the road and ascend the footpath turning left at the T along the wooded path behind Warden Park School. The walk continues past the pond to enter Holy Trinity cemetery on the left. Continue to the right of Church into Cuckfield high street. Turn right and continue along London Lane then right into Polestub Lane passing the Baptist Church and up the footpath to Ardingly Road continuing right past Horsefield Green. At the zebra crossing follow the footpath sign pointing right along Longacre Crescent into the track. After the metal gate, keep straight ignoring the half right fork and continue straight through the copse ahead. After the pond and gate keep straight, also at the grass path cross roads and, as directed by a public footpath sign, roughly straight over the dog gated . After the gate of Gravelye House continue straight down through the wood then up and, in 2020 following a diversion due to building work for new houses, back into the wood keeping its fence to your right which eventually follows the grounds of Harlands School where the footpath exits into Penlands Road. Cross into the path across the road down into Barnsmead. Turn right then continue right along to Balcombe Road to pass under the railway bridge. Turn right up Mill Green Road ascending to the roundabout and beyond. Head right through the car park to the Cricket Pavilion and continue right on the path through the heath to Heath Road.

Cross the road and continue along the footpath next to the car park into Church Road and then into Orchards car park.

5.6 mile/9km

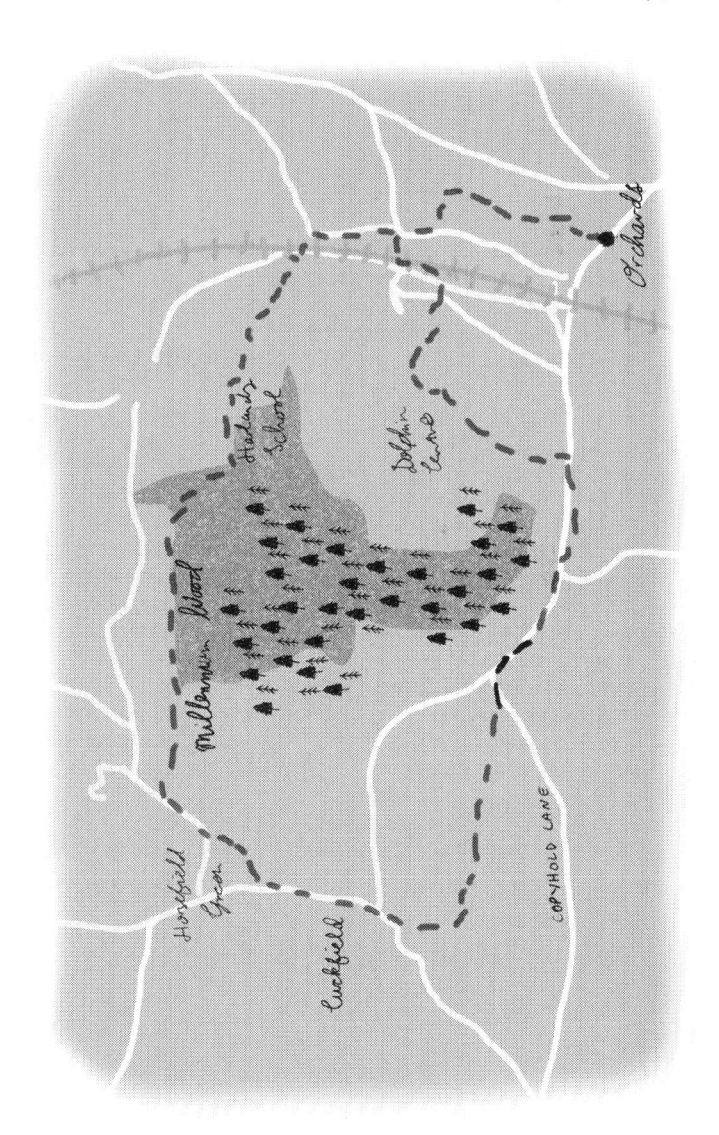

Walstead

> Snowdrop Lane one way and Snowflake Lane the other 'lighten' this 6 mile circular walk to Walstead

Snowdrops: Theirs is a fragile but hardy celebration in the very teeth of winter. Louise Wilder

From Orchards car park descend through the precinct and turn left along South Road. Continue to the roundabout and turn left down Caxton Way continuing straight ahead down the Syresham Gardens footpath beside the stream to St Augustine's Way. Turn right then left along Priory Way to Western Road. Turn left and cross the road into the footpath down to the left of the Cemetery gates. Continue left on the path at the bottom of the graveyard then right into Silver Birches, left into The Hollow and walk on to No. 2 ascend the track to Gravelye Lane, turn right and cross the road into Lyoth Lane. Continue up the steep narrow road to Snowdrop Lane and turn left walking past Snowdrop Inn on a beautiful country lane to its junction with the B2111 Lewes Road. Cross diagonally following the footpath sign through into a narrow path along a field. At the end enter a farm track continuing to a . After the enter a large field. Walk sharp left heading for another accessing the footpath through Walstead Place Farm. Continue past cottages on your right following the path across an access road into another field and then across East Mascalls Lane into Snowflake Lane, the road to Walstead Forge, which narrows into a footpath afterwards. This section can be muddy after rain. Continue in the same direction to the footpath junction taking the left turn towards Lindfield. Continue straight ignoring the right turn for Lindfield village following the path between fields which enters Bancroft Drive. Head right down the Drive, cross Newton Road and proceed down Luxford Road and Eastern Road to Lewes Road. Cross into Lindfield Common recreation ground heading straight towards the tennis courts and then left into the access footpath at the field corner. Cross Meadow Drive into the next stretch of footpath passing over Scrase stream into William Allen Lane. Enter Scrase Valley Local Nature Reserve continuing with the stream to your right.

Turn left at the junction walking up and across to Barn Cottage Lane. After the recreation ground, turn right up New England Road to Hazelgrove Road. Cross to Church Road and Orchards.

5.8 miles/9.3 km

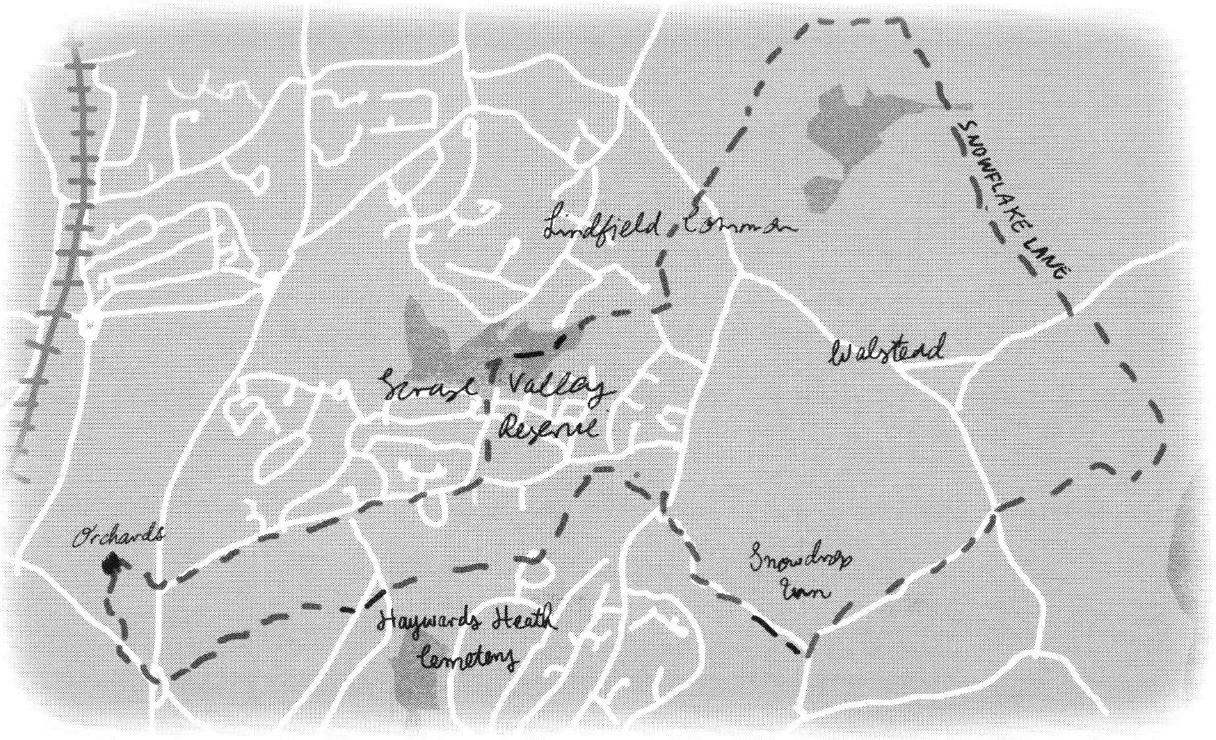
SNOWFLAKE LANE
Lindfield Common
Walstead
Scrase Valley Reserve
Orchards
Snowdrop Inn
Haywards Heath Cemetery

Ardingly College

> 7 mile walk across Haywards Heath Golf Course through River's Wood to Ardingly College returning by bus

The truth cannot impose itself except by virtue of its own truth, as it makes its entrance into the mind at once quietly and with power.
Second Vatican Council

Ardingly College boarding and day independent school has a pelican on its logo. Pelicans in legend feeding their young from their own blood are in Christian symbolism pointers to the eucharist central to the Anglo-Catholic tradition of schools such as Ardingly, Hurstpierpoint and Lancing in Sussex which are members of the Woodard Corporation. The Chapel - well worth a visit - and its Bell Tower are prominent on the High Weald sky line visible to railway passengers crossing Balcombe Viaduct to and from London. In turn pupils at the School profit from the inspirational views provided from the thoughtful location of the school buildings. Old Ardinians include satirist Ian Hislop, actor Terry Thomas and Formula One World Champion Mike Hawthorn.

From Orchards car park go up to Church Road and turn right. Cross Hazelgrove Road and turn right heading left down New England Road. After the shops turn left along Barn Cottage Lane with the recreation ground to your right. Cross Hanbury Lane and continue down the path between the houses into Scrase Valley Reserve. After 200 yards turn right at the junction and follow the Scrase stream on your left. Exit the Reserve into Croxton Lane keeping the stream to your left and cross the bridge on the advertised public footpath into Meadow Drive. Cross the Drive to continue on the footpath opposite which leads to the tennis courts at the southern corner of Lindfield Common recreation ground. Continue diagonally across the field to enter Lindfield High Street. Head past All Saints Church and turn left before the right bend entering the footpath running behind the houses. This path ends on Finches Lane. Turn right and follow the track through the woods to a junction with the road into Kenwards Farm. Turn left to the main road and cross into the wood straight up the path which follows the edge of the field then zig zags through the trees. Turn right at the fork then right again at a second fork which veers left continuing on the old railway embankment near Copyhold Lane. At its end descend carefully to the footpath and go through the gate on your right. Cross the Lane diagonally to your right into the footpath to River's Farm and continue through River's Wood. Cross the stream and follow the steep path upwards then half right through a field and the Reservoir comes into sight. Turn right on arrival at the Activity Centre heading to the water works and bear left. At the top of the road turn left at the standing footpath sign past Ardingly Pre-Prep School.

Turn right at the grass island heading up to the main school bearing right in front of St Saviour's Chapel to the main entrance. Cross the road passing through the sports facilities into the wood. Continue straight ahead. Exit the wood crossing the meadow to the footpath junction sign. Turn left and continue along the footpath through the fields into the hedged path and metalled track to the main road. Turn left along the pavement. Cross to catch the 272 Orchards at the bus stop diagonally opposite Hapstead Hall.

6.5 mile/10.4 km

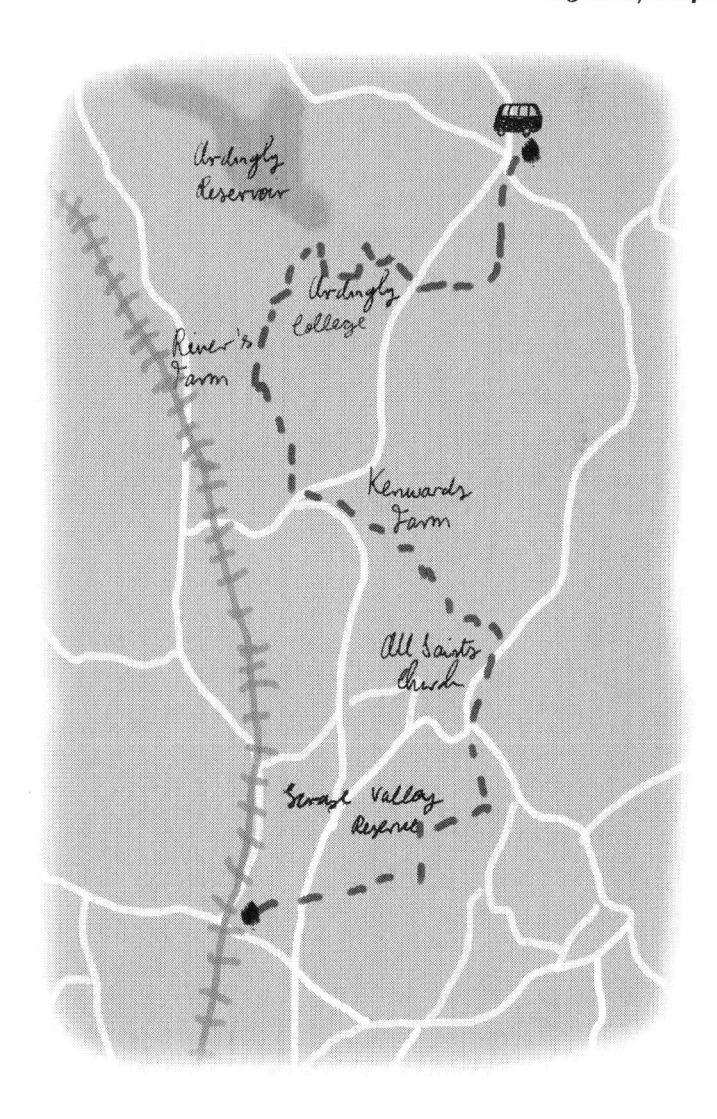

33 Wakehurst Place

> 7 mile walk via Haywards Heath Golf Course and Ardingly Reservoir to Wakehurst Place returning by bus

The kingdom of heaven is like a mustard seed that someone took and sowed in his field; it is the smallest of all the seeds, but when it has grown it is the greatest of shrubs and becomes a tree, so that the birds of the air come and make nests in its branches. Jesus Christ

Wakehurst's Millennium Seed Bank (2000) is run by Kew Gardens who collaborate with the National Trust in providing public access to the Bank alongside the Tudor mansion (1590) and extensive gardens owned by the Trust but managed by Kew. The Bank collects and conserves seeds from all of the UK's native flora and much of the world's flora to save species from extinction in the wild. The early 20th century gardens are among the largest in the UK at 490 acres and include walled and water gardens, woodland and wetland conservation areas. In among the colours and variety of the trees stand a handful of bare trunks deriving from the great storm of 1987. Dead and hollow they were kept to serve as bat roosts. Wakehurst has the largest growing Christmas tree in England, a 35 metre (115ft) redwood lit in season by 1,800 lights. The footpath from the south crosses the famous Ardingly Showground.

Go up to Church Road from Orchards car park and turn right. Cross Hazelgrove Road and turn right heading left down New England Road. After the shops turn left along Barn Cottage Lane with the recreation ground to your right. Cross Hanbury Lane and continue down the path between the houses into Scrase Valley Reserve. After 200 yards turn right at the junction and follow the Scrase stream on your left. Exit the Reserve into Croxton Lane keeping the stream to your left and cross the bridge on the advertised public footpath into Meadow Drive. Cross the Drive to continue on the footpath opposite which leads to the tennis courts at the southern corner of Lindfield Common recreation ground. Continue diagonally across the field to enter Lindfield High Street. Head past All Saints Church and turn left before the right bend entering the footpath running behind the houses. This path ends on Finches Lane. Turn right and follow the track through the woods to a junction with the road into Kenwards Farm. Turn left to the main road and cross with care into the wood straight up the path which follows the edge of the field then zig zags through the trees. Turn right at the fork, then right again at a second fork which veers left continuing on the old railway embankment near Copyhold Lane. At its end descend carefully to the footpath and go through the gate on your right. Walk across the Lane diagonally to the right and descend the footpath to River's Farm continuing through River's Wood.

Cross the stream and follow the steep path upwards then half right through a field to the Reservoir. Walk along its bank and turn left into the walking trail. After the wooded section take a right turn going over a . Walk up the fields into Church Lane, Ardingly. At the top of the Lane at St Peter's Church, Ardingly turn right then left into the Showground footpath which continues alongside the grounds then further north to Wakehurst Place. Access to the shop, restaurant and toilet is free. Catch the 272 bus back to Orchards or arrange a lift back to Haywards Heath.

6.7 miles/10.7 km

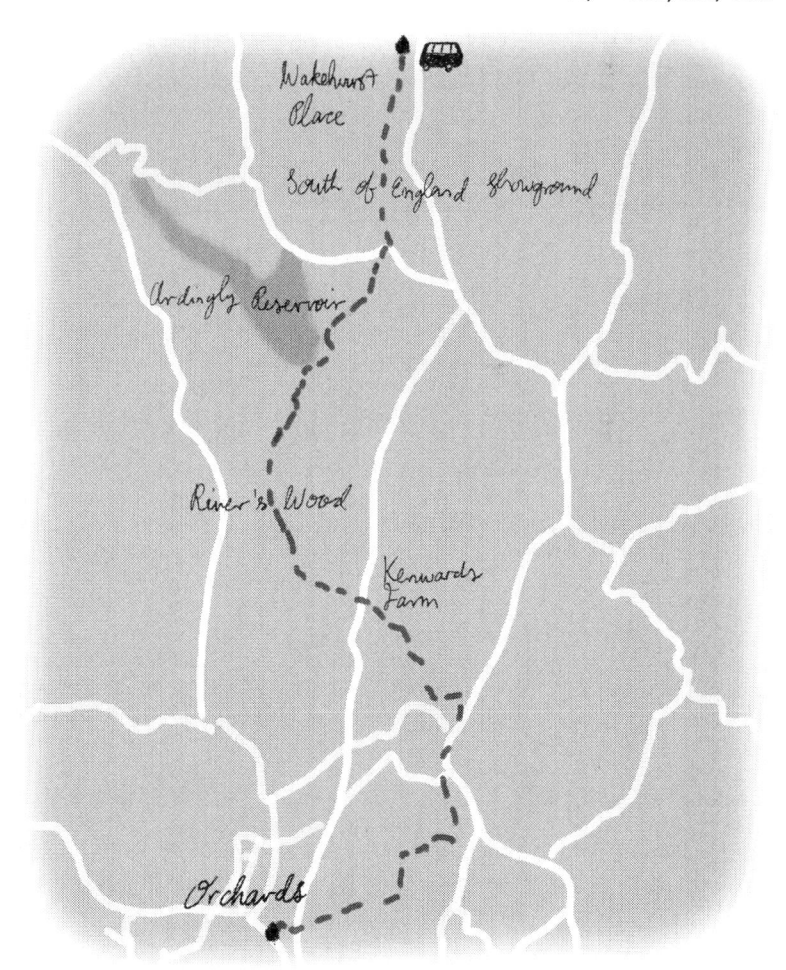

34   Ardingly Reservoir

> 7 mile walk across Haywards Heath Golf Course to Ardingly Reservoir returning by bus

It is the small things in life which count; it is the inconsequential leak which empties the biggest reservoir. Charles Comiskey

The River Ouse skirts Haywards Heath on its way from Lower Beeding to Newhaven. In 1978, following expansion of the local population with increased demand for water, it was decided to dam Shell Brook, tributary of the Ouse, and create Ardingly Reservoir. With capacity over 5000 million litres it is filled with water pumped from the Ouse when it flows high. The Reservoir Centre facilitates water sports including windsurfing, canoeing, powerboating and dinghy sailing. Viewing the water level is a walker's hobby. In River's Wood the walk crosses the disused line from Haywards Heath to Ardingly of interest to Bluebell Railway. On leaving the wood Balcombe viaduct is visible to the left.

From Orchards car park go up to Church Road and turn right. Cross Hazelgrove Road and turn right heading left down New England Road. After the shops turn left along Barn Cottage Lane with the recreation ground to your right. Cross Hanbury Lane and continue down the path between the houses into Scrase Valley Reserve. After 200 yards turn right at the junction and follow the Scrase stream on your left. Exit the Reserve into Croxton Lane keeping the stream to your left and cross the bridge on the advertised public footpath into Meadow Drive. Cross the Drive to continue on the footpath opposite which leads to the tennis courts at the southern corner of Lindfield Common recreation ground. Continue diagonally across the field to enter Lindfield High Street. Head past All Saints Church and turn left before the right bend entering the footpath running behind the houses. This path ends on Finches Lane. Turn right and follow the track through the woods to a junction with the road into Kenwards Farm. Turn left to the main road and cross into the wood straight up the path which follows the edge of the field then zig zags through the trees. Turn right at the fork then right again at a second fork which veers left continuing on the old railway embankment near Copyhold Lane. At its end descend carefully to the footpath and go through the gate on your right. Walk across the Lane diagonally to the right and descend the footpath to River's Farm continuing through River's Wood. Cross the stream and follow the steep path upwards then half right through a field to the Reservoir. Walk along its bank and at the end turn left into the Reservoir walking trail entering a wooded section. After this take a right turn going over a . Walk up the fields into Church Lane, Ardingly. At the top of the Lane on the left view Grade 1 listed St Peter's Church, built 14th century in the Decorated Gothic style.

Turn right and continue to the Hapstead Hall bus stop at the end of the road for the 272 Orchards bus.

6.9 mile/11.1 km

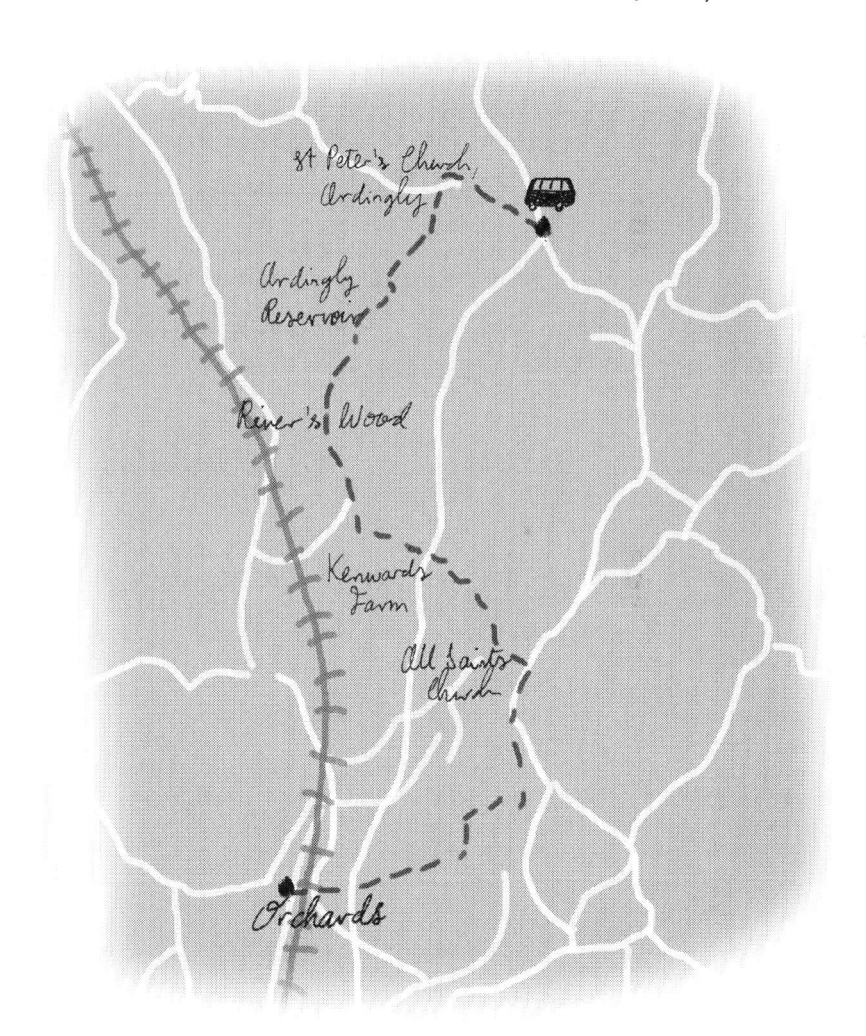

35 Heaven

> 8 mile walk to Heaven Farm returning by bus from Danehill

Awesome, intriguing sights that point beyond themselves. John Twisleton

From Orchards car park descend through the precinct and turn left along South Road. Continue down to the roundabout and turn left down Caxton Way continuing straight ahead down the Syresham Gardens footpath beside the stream to St Augustine's Way. Turn right then left along Priory Way to Western Road. Turn left and cross the road into the footpath down to the left of the Cemetery gates. Continue left at the bottom of the graveyard then right into Silver Birches, left into The Hollow and walk on to No. 2. Go up the track to Gravelye Lane and cross diagonally in effect to enter Lyoth Lane. Continue up the steep narrow road to Snowdrop Lane and turn left walking to its junction with the B2111 Lewes Road. Cross diagonally following the footpath sign through into a narrow path along a field. At the end enter a farm track continuing to a . After the enter a large field and cross straight ahead to enter the wood. Follow the footpath through the woods, which eventually runs parallel to overhead cables, up to Scaynes Hill Common on Church Road. Turn left and take the right hand track continuing between hedges to a gate opening into a field. Cross the field to a gate by a pond. Follow the path along going through a hedge into another field. After the gate, turn left to walk down the road. Take the footpath on your left skirting the farm buildings descending across a large field to another gate. Head left through a copse skirting a wooden fence. At the buildings head left through a wooden gate going on to cross a . Turn right down to the main road, left past the Sloop Inn and join Sussex Border Path (SBP) to your right at the farm drive. Cross a large field heading for a metal gate then turn left under the Bluebell Railway bridge, left again as directed along the edge of the fields then right and left into Kings Wood. You arrive at Ketches Lane beside the stream and West Sussex sign. Turn right along the road and rejoin SBP turning left for Northland. Keep right at the farm continuing around the grounds, as signs indicate, then through a wood and right into a field, along the side of a wood. At the corner of the field cross a gate with into the trees. After a short distance pass through a metal gate down the field to your left to Heaven Farm with its cafeteria. Walk on to the A275, turn left and left again into Church Lane. After All Saints Church you rejoin A275. Walk on to the top of School Lane for the 270 bus stop to return to Orchards.

7.8 mile/12.5 km

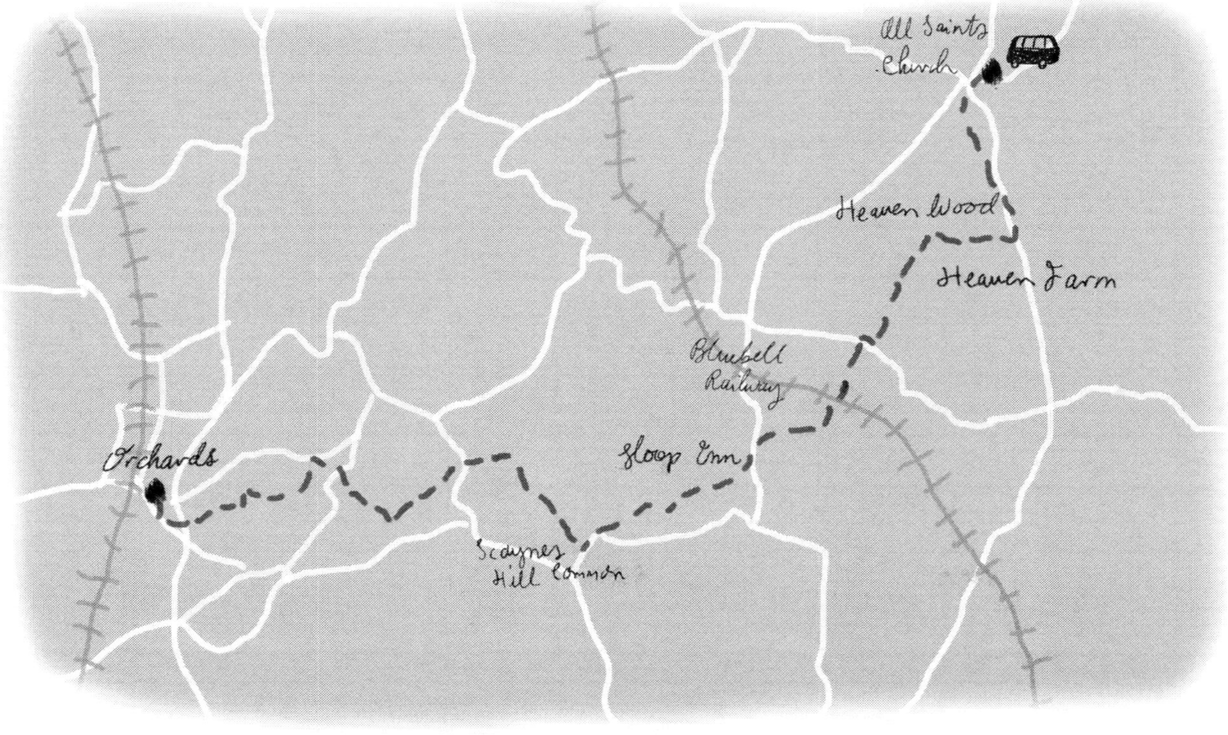

All Saints Church
Heaven Wood
Heaven Farm
Bluebell Railway
Sloop Inn
Scaynes Hill Common
Orchards

Balcombe

> 8 mile walk to Balcombe returning by train

I needed to commit and focus my inner understanding and strength outside myself. Brian Keenan, former hostage

Like Haywards Heath, Balcombe gained fame through the London-Brighton railway which required a viaduct to cross the River Ouse Valley. The viaduct, completed 1841 in Italianate style, has 11 million bricks which were carried by barge along the Ouse from Scaynes Hill. This process required construction of extra canal cuttings to avoid bends in the river as alongside The Sloop Inn at Scaynes Hill. The arches were tapered to reduce the number of bricks needed in construction, an impressive sight from under the viaduct. Balcombe village, surrounded by woods and lakes, has the beautiful St Mary's Church and a good number of listed buildings.

From Orchards car park head up to Church Road and turn right. Cross Hazelgrove Road and turn right heading left down New England Road. After the shops turn left along Barn Cottage Lane with the recreation ground to your right. Cross Hanbury Lane and continue down the path between the houses into Scrase Valley Reserve. After 200 yards turn right at the junction and follow the Scrase stream on your left. Exit the Reserve into Croxton Lane keeping the stream to your left and cross the bridge on the advertised public footpath into Meadow Drive. Cross the Drive to continue on the footpath opposite which leads to the tennis courts at the southern corner of Lindfield Common recreation ground. Continue diagonally across the field to enter Lindfield High Street. Head past All Saints Church and turn left before the right bend entering the footpath running behind the houses. This path ends on Finches Lane. Turn right and follow the track through the woods to a junction with the road into Kenwards Farm. Turn left to the main road and cross into the wood straight up the path which follows the edge of the field then zig zags through the trees. Turn right at the fork, then right again at a second fork which veers left, continuing on the old railway embankment near Copyhold Lane. At its end descend carefully to the footpath and go through the gate on your right. Walk across the Lane diagonally to the right and descend the footpath to River's Farm continuing through River's Wood. Cross the stream and follow the steep path upwards, where you briefly see Balcombe Viaduct in the distance on your left. At the top head half right through a field and then a gate to the Reservoir. Walk along its bank and at the end turn left into the waterside walking trail taking you along the eastern side of the Reservoir. The trail passes over a road bridge returns to the lake and rises back on to the road where you walk on crossing a bridge and then ascend a stepped footpath on your left. After the top gate continue straight up the field on the left of the wood, then through a gate into a bridle path to the road and turn left along the pavement.

Take the first right along Oldlands Avenue continuing to the cutting on the left down to the main road. Descend to Balcombe Station returning by train over the viaduct to Haywards Heath Station.

8 mile/12.9 km

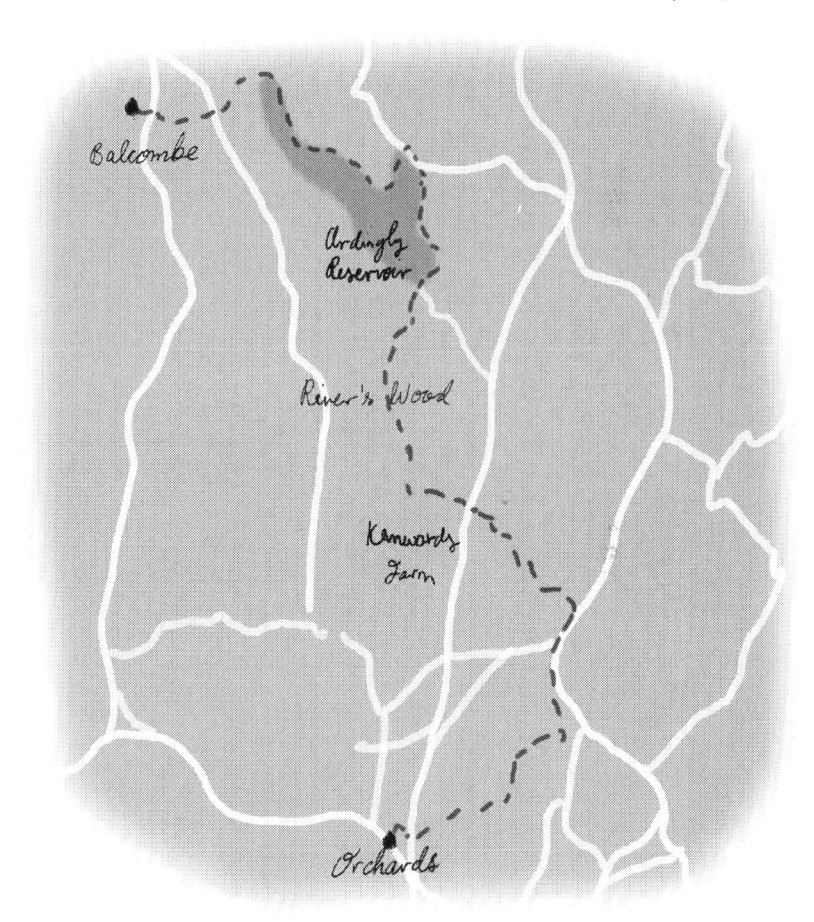

Ditchling

> 8 mile walk to Ditchling via the Sussex Border Path returning by bus from Keymer

Some people see things as they are and say 'Why?'. I dream things that never were and say 'why not?' George Bernard Shaw

Go down the precinct from Orchards car park and turn left along South Road. Continue down to the roundabout and turn left down Caxton Way continuing straight ahead down the Syresham Gardens footpath beside the stream to St Augustine's Way. Turn right then left along Priory Way to Western Road. Turn left and cross the road into the footpath down to the left of the Cemetery gates. Continue left at the bottom of the graveyard then right into Silver Birches, left into The Hollow and walk on to No. 2. Go up the track to Gravelye Lane and cross diagonally in effect to enter Lyoth Lane. Continue up the steep narrow road to Snowdrop Lane, turn right and walk to Lewes Road. Cross the road. Turn left to walk carefully along the verge turning right after a distance into Slugwash Lane descending to Wivelsfield Green where you cross the main road into Eastern Road opposite. Continue past the village hall round the right bend and left as signed along the lane before the houses. At the end of this lane enter the bridleway through West Wood ignoring paths to right or left aided by Border Path signs. Exit onto a track with houses continuing to the road. Turn right crossing at the top of Spatham Lane into the footpath along the edge of a field. After a gate, turn left over a into a large field heading left to cross the railway. Take the path on the left down the field crossing s into a copse following the path into a field. Continue down over a bridge bearing right along the path then left through the into a narrow path which opens into a field. Continue over two s into another narrow path opening into a field. Go through a wooden gate to a sign posted 'dog leg' in the path, left then right. Continue past the pond to a and on to rejoin the Border Path. Go straight ahead through two farm gates past Mac's Farm across a lane then over a followed by a right turn over a into a field crossing left to climb over another . Head right passing through two gates, left down East Gardens and left into Ditchling. The 31 Orchards bus leaves Ockley Lane, Keymer (30min walk) or arrange a lift.

8.3 mile/13.4 km

Orchards

SLUGWASH LANE

Windlesfield Green

West Wood

Mac's Farm

Ditchling

38 Borde Hill

> 8 mile circular walk via Lindfield to Borde Hill returning via Blunts Wood

No one frees anyone. No one achieves freedom alone. Human beings achieve freedom in communion. Paolo Freire

From Orchards car park go up to Church Road and turn right. Cross Hazelgrove Road and turn right heading left down New England Road. After the shops turn left along Barn Cottage Lane. Cross Hanbury Lane and continue down the path between the houses into Scrase Valley Reserve. Turn right at the junction and follow the Scrase stream on your left. Exit into Croxton Lane and continue crossing the bridge into Meadow Drive then passing across to the footpath opposite which leads to the tennis courts on Lindfield Common. Continue diagonally across the field to enter Lindfield High Street. Head past All Saints Church and turn left before the right bend entering the footpath running behind the houses leading to Finches Lane. Turn right and follow the track through the woods to a junction with the road into Kenwards Farm. Turn left to the main road and cross with care into the wood, straight up the path which follows the edge of the field then zig zags through the trees. Turn right at the fork, then right again at a second fork, which veers left continuing on the old railway embankment near Copyhold Lane. At its end descend carefully to the footpath and go through the gate onto the Lane. Turn left continuing over the bridge and view the Ardingly rail junction on the right. At the road junction cross and turn left following the sign for Borde Hill Gardens. After 200 yards turn right following footpath signs for High Weald Landscape Trail past the Garden entrance. The trail continues over a cattle grate then left following the road through Stone Lodge. After Lullings Farm go straight across the road junction. At the top cross the main road and turn right. At the roundabout turn left, and then left diagonally across the grass after the bus stop, to enter the path to the right of the housing. Walk down to the metal gate and enter the field. Follow the footpath signed half right down to a standing T junction signpost and turn right. Go through the gate and head left down the field towards the barn-like building at Horsgate Farm. Cross the and continue past that building walking down then up Horsgate Lane emerging opposite the Wheatsheaf Pub. Turn left and left again down Hatchgate Lane. Walk straight ahead at the bottom continuing along the hedged path into Paige's North Meadow and through Blunts Wood. At the car park head right along the pavement of Bluntswood Crescent. Turn left into Bluntswood Road and then right along Lucastes Avenue continuing to the footpath sign. Follow the path to the left. Continue keeping right at the junction to walk behind the Leisure Centre up to Milton Road. Turn right then and, with care, left at the end of the railings to the traffic island.

Cross again, walk down to cross Boltro Road and turn left walking past the station side entrance. Continue under the railway bridge across the main station entrance and turn right at the roundabout. Cross Perrymount Road into the car park and walk diagonally up to the Cricket Pavilion, keeping right through the ancient heath to Heath Road. Cross the road and continue along the footpath next to the car park into Church Road and then through either St Joseph's or St Wilfrid's Way into Orchards car park.

8.3 mile/13.4 km

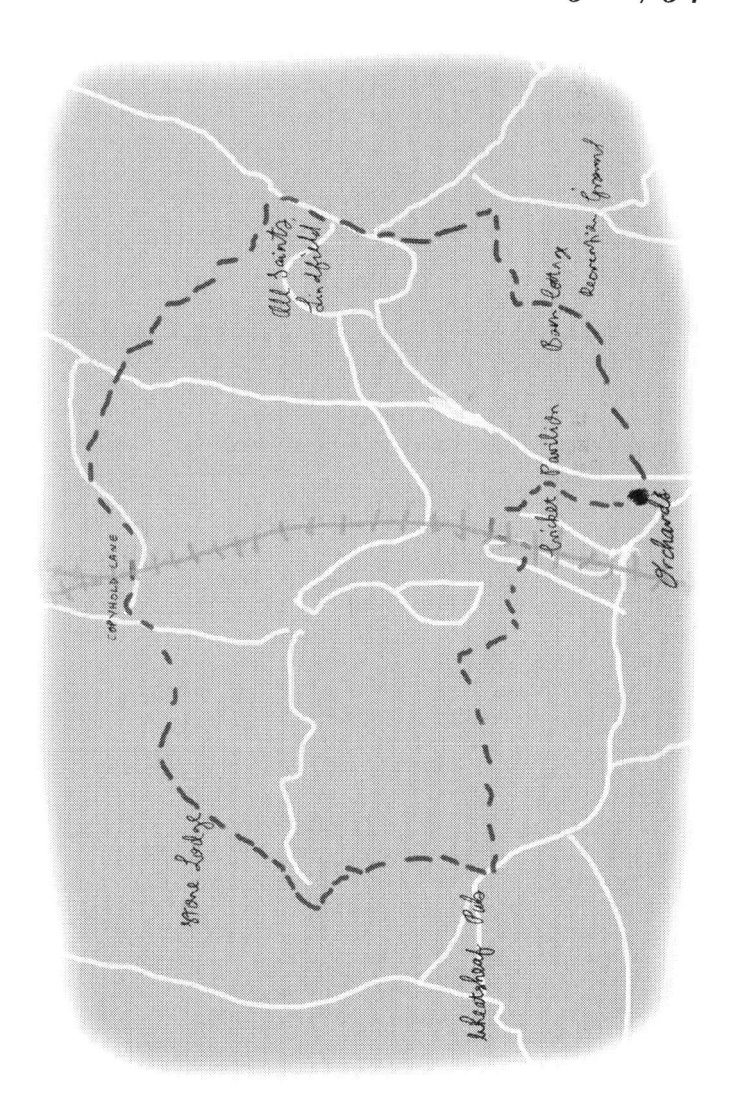

39   Scaynes Hill

> 9 mile circular walk via Walstead to Scaynes Hill returning via Sussex Border Path and Slugwash Lane

Oh! The Downs high to the cool sky; and the feel of the sun-warmed moss; and each cardoon [thistle], like a full moon, fairy-spun of the thistle floss; and the beech grove, and a wood-dove, and the trail where the shepherds pass; and the lark's song, and then wind-song, and then scent of the parching grass! John Galsworthy

Galsworthy's praise of the South Downs captures the exhilaration walking south from Haywards Heath where they stretch across the horizon.

Descend through the shopping precinct from Orchards car park and turn left along South Road. Continue down to the roundabout and turn left down Caxton Way, continuing straight ahead down the Syresham Gardens footpath beside the stream to St Augustine's Way. Turn right then left along Priory Way to Western Road. Turn left and cross the road into the footpath down to the left of the Cemetery gates. Continue left at the bottom of the graveyard, then right into Silver Birches, left into The Hollow and walk on to No. 2. Go up the track to Gravelye Lane and cross diagonally in effect to enter Lyoth Lane. Continue up the steep narrow road to Snowdrop Lane and turn left walking to its junction with the B2111 Lewes Road. Cross diagonally following the footpath sign through into a narrow path along a field. At the end enter a farm track continuing to a . After the , enter a large field and cross straight ahead to enter the wood. Follow the footpath through the woods, which eventually runs parallel to overhead cables, up to Scaynes Hill Common on Church Road. Turn right and walk up to the petrol station. Cross into the footpath to the right of The Farmers Pub. Continue across the road and straight ahead at the junction directed by the West Sussex Border Path (SBP) sign. Cross the next road down the tarmac way and follow down. Continue in the same direction turning left at the T junction. Go past Ham Lane Farm above which a wide view of the South Downs opens with wooded foreground. After the left bend take the right hand turn as signed, continuing past Hooters Garage down the path in the same direction towards the pond, entering the wood on the left. Descend across the road along to a with a dog gate into a field. Cross to another stile and dog gate into a narrow footpath which crosses a stream and passes along through a copse where you might see pheasants. This section can be muddy. Ascend under the pylons to a junction following repeated SBP signs to emerge past Slugwash Kennels onto Slugwash Lane. Turn right and walk up to Lewes Road. Turn left to walk along the verge and path before crossing the road into Snowdrop Lane. Take the left turn signed for Lyoth Lane. At the bottom of the lane cross Gravelye Lane to pass down the track diagonally opposite into America Lane.

Walk up New England Road crossing into Church Road and Orchards car park.

8.6 mile/13.8 km

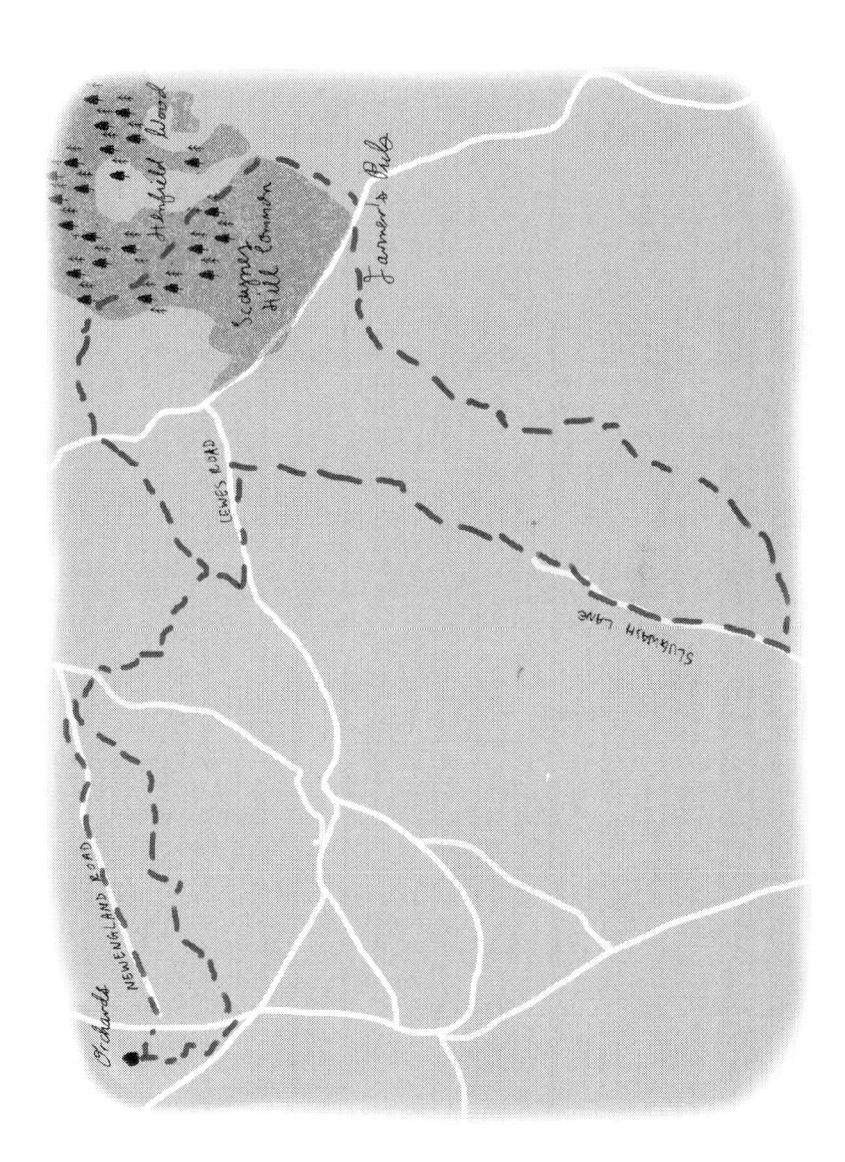

Birch Grove

> 9 mile walk through Horsted Keynes to Chelwood Gate returning by bus

It's a good thing to be laughed at. It's better than to be ignored.
Harold Macmillan

Former Prime Minister Harold Macmillan and his wife Dorothy lived at Birch Grove House and were well known in Chelwood Gate, Danehill, Forest Row and Horsted Keynes. Macmillan combined his national role with hunting, shooting, reading theology and attending St Giles, Horsted Keynes sometimes twice on a Sunday. When one of his most famous visitors, President John Kennedy, was assassinated in 1963 he insisted the reading in St Giles the following Sunday be changed to 'Let us now praise famous men'. Kennedy attended Mass in neighbouring Forest Row months before his death. Macmillan's own death brought drama to Horsted Keynes. On funeral day sharp shooters were placed on the roofs in Church Lane to guarantee the safety of Macmillan's more turbulent successor, Prime Minister Margaret Thatcher who led a contingent of celebrity mourners in St Giles.

Head up to Church Road from Orchards car park and turn right. Cross Hazelgrove Road and turn right heading left down New England Road. After the shops turn left along Barn Cottage Lane with the recreation ground to your right. Cross Hanbury Lane and continue down the path between the houses into Scrase Valley Reserve. After 200 yards turn right at the junction and follow the Scrase stream on your left. Exit the Reserve into Croxton Lane keeping the stream to your left and cross the bridge on the advertised public footpath into Meadow Drive. Cross the Drive to continue on the footpath opposite which leads into Lindfield recreation ground. Walk across the field aiming in between the seats off Lewes Road. Cross ditch and road to enter Eastern Road turning left up Luxford Road and then Barncroft Drive. As the Drive veers right turn left into the footpath. Continue straight ahead with a large field on your left until the T at a fence. Turn right and continue in the same direction ignoring the right turn crossing two stiles before walking along the River Ouse on your left to the road. Turn left walking past East Mascalls Farm and the Paxhill Park Golf Course to the wood. Leave the road ascending the path to your right leading into a large field. Cross the field back to the road, along which the path continues briefly to Cockhaise Farm. Turn left here along a track. Take a half right turn along a footpath which descends to cross Bluebell Railway and then skirts below Tremaines Manor to the road. Turn left and walk into Horsted Keynes turning right along Lewes Road to reach the village green. If you have time, walk down to St Giles Church where the Macmillan grave is found with its Celtic Cross beyond the yew tree at the east end of the building. From the village green walk keeping the Green Man pub to your left.

Go round the left bend, continuing along Birch Grove Road past Westall House, carefully round a sharp left bend and then gentler right bend. Continue the more or less straight country lane which passes Birch Grove House on the right. The road bends right after crossing Danehill brook continuing to the A275 Lewes Road. Catch the 270 Orchards bus from outside the Red Lion pub on this road junction.

8.6 mile/13.8 km

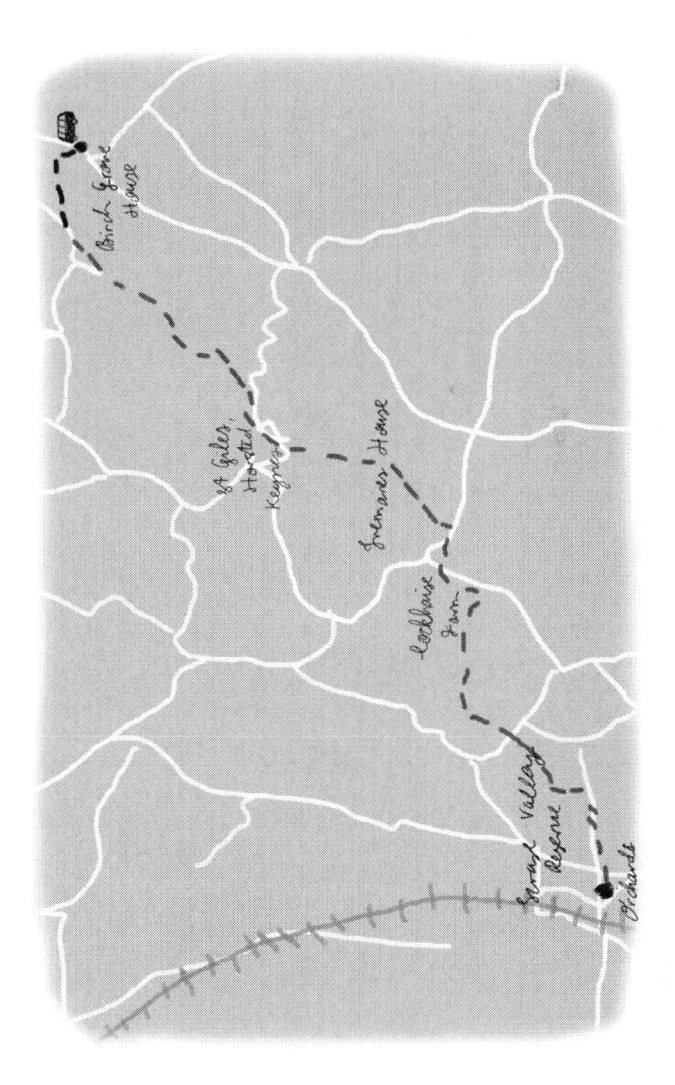

Paxhill Park

> 9 mile circular walk to historic Paxhill Park

I would like to be remembered as someone who did very little harm. Most people do a great deal of harm. Paul Eddington

Head up to Church Road from Orchards car park and turn right. Cross Hazelgrove Road, turn right then head left down New England Road. After the shops turn left along Barn Cottage Lane with the recreation ground to your right. Cross Hanbury Lane and continue down the path between the houses into Scrase Valley Reserve. After 200 yards turn right at the junction and follow the Scrase stream on your left. Exit the Reserve into Croxton Lane keeping the stream to your left and cross the bridge on the advertised public footpath into Meadow Drive. Cross the Drive to continue on the footpath opposite which leads into Lindfield Common recreation ground. Walk across the field aiming in between the seats off Lewes Road. Cross ditch and road to enter Eastern Road turning left up Luxford Road and then Barncroft Drive. As the Drive veers right turn left into the footpath. Continue straight ahead with a large field on your left until the T at a fence. Turn right and continue ignoring the right turn. The chimneys of Paxhill Park (1606) tower above the trees. Keeping in the same direction cross two stiles before walking with the River Ouse on your left to the road. At the road cross and view the weir and pond. Turn left and after the manor enter the footpath on your left which passes in front of Lindfield Golf Clubhouse. Follow the path which exits the Golf Course over a bridge. Turn left up the field, through one gate then another by the house, into the signed footpath. Walk on as the park opens up before you and the turreted splendour of Paxhill Park mansion to your right. Head left along the footpath down the meadow continuing to the road. Turn left to walk to the bridge over the River Ouse where there is a seat. Cross the road continuing on footpath then pavement into Lindfield High Street. Turn right onto the footpath opposite The Tiger beside the Bower House. Walk on past the Vicarage to Hickmans Lane and cross into the Recreation Ground. Head past the left side of the pavilion, to the willow trees and the cutting behind them, into Pickers Green. Go straight past the roundabout to the end of the road turning right down the footpath into Hickmans Lane. Cross into Sunte Avenue continuing to the roundabout and enter the footpath to Old Wickham Lane from where you turn left into Wickham Way descending to College Road with St Wilfrid's on the horizon. Cross College Road, turn right and immediately left up Mill Green Road ascending to the roundabout and straight across. Walk to the left across the car park to the Cricket Pavilion and continue right on the path through the heath to Heath Road. Cross the road and continue along the footpath next to the car park into Church Road and then into Orchards car park.

8.6 mile/13.9 km

Paxhill Manor

River Ouse

BANCROFT DELVE

Beeney's Farm

Lindfield Common

Scrase Valley Reserve

Orchards

Haywards Heath Railway Station

Wivelsfield Church

> 9 mile circular walk down Slugwash Lane to Wivelsfield Church returning via Colwell Lane

The question which divides people today is whether Society will be merely an immense exploitation for the benefit of the strongest or a consecration of everyone for the service of all. Frederick Ozanam

From Orchards car park descend through the precinct and turn left along South Road. Continue down to the roundabout and turn left down Caxton Way, continuing straight ahead down the Syresham Gardens footpath beside the stream to St Augustine's Way. Turn right then left along Priory Way to Western Road. Turn left and cross the road into the footpath down to the left of the Cemetery gates. Continue left at the bottom of the graveyard, then right into Silver Birches, left into The Hollow and walk on to No. 2. Go up the track to Gravelye Lane and cross diagonally, in effect, to enter Lyoth Lane. Continue up the steep narrow road to Snowdrop Lane, turn right and walk to Lewes Road. Cross the road with care. Turn left to walk along the path and verge, turning right after a distance into Slugwash Lane. After Slugwash Kennels follow the bends in the road. At the top of the hill, after the safety mirrors opposite Townings Place and before the White House, turn right onto the footpath through the wooden gate and proceed along a fence then hedge on your right, then heading half left to a gate. Head across the large field to the right of the water tank and housing development towards the gate in the gap in the trees. Proceed along the concrete track beyond the gate crossing the stile on your left then walking across the field to the main road. Cross the B2112 to the Haywards Heath bus stop and take the path just beyond it across the field. At the metal gate take the right hand path to the Churchyard. Walk up past the Church turning left at the road heading for Lunces Hall and take the right hand kissing gate. At the junction with steps turn right and continue as the path steers to the right along the hedge to join the farm road beyond the metal gate in the field corner. Continue passing under the pylon cables past Griggs Farmhouse along a concrete road, dropping off that to the left after the house, passing to the Haywards Heath sign on the main road. Follow the pavement to the Fox & Hounds. Cross there to Hurstwood Lane continuing on the pavement then footpath until the junction sign. Turn right into Colwell Lane and after the houses proceed up the wide path which joins a tarmac road for the ascent to Lewes Road. Turn right there along the pavement passing Birch Close opposite. Cross Lewes Road at the footpath signs to descend a narrow path. Cross Cobbetts Mead and continue down the path opposite emerging between two large hedges into The Oaks. Follow the footpath sign down the next stretch of path which ends with a rustic fence leading into Lyoth Lane. Turn left, and at the bottom of the lane cross Gravelye Lane to pass down the track diagonally opposite, into America Lane.

Walk up New England Road crossing Hazelgrove Road into Church Road and Orchards car park.

8.8 mile/14.1 km

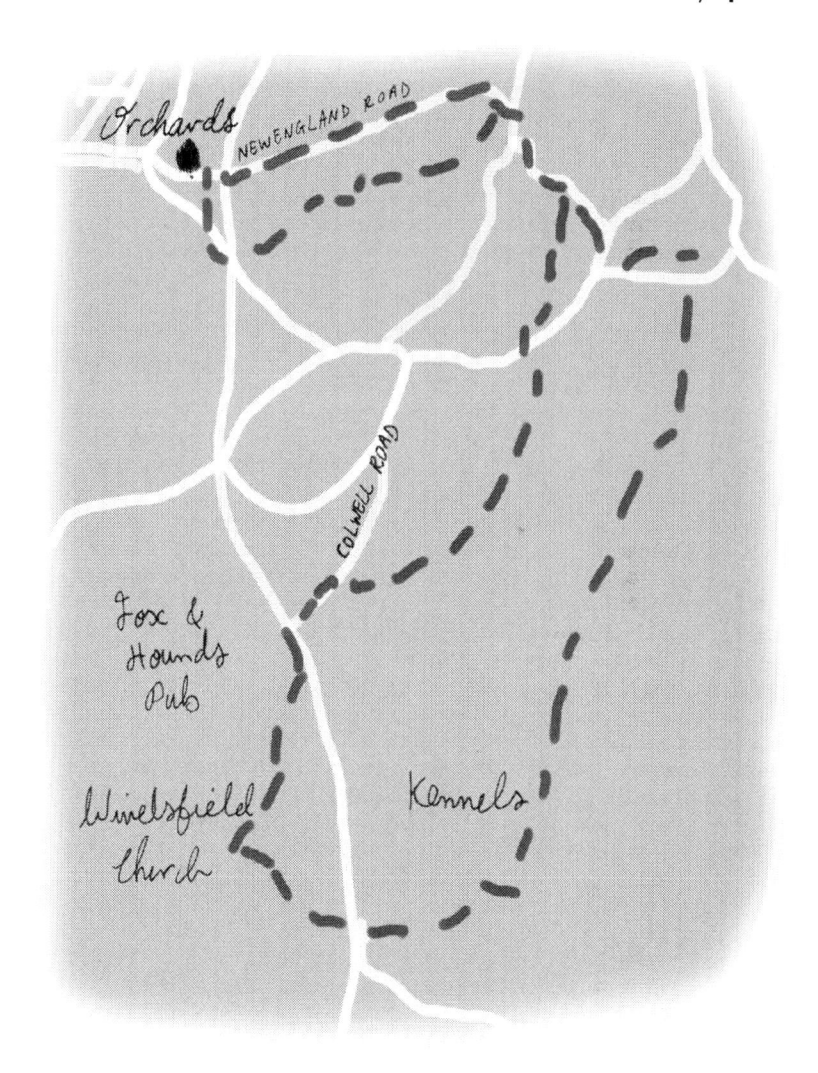

43   Buxshalls

> 9 mile circular walk through Lindfield to Buxshalls House returning via East Mascalls

Yesterday is history, tomorrow is a mystery, today is a gift - which is why it's called the present. Anon

Buxshalls House (1830s) was once seat of the Asquith family. Its white facade catches the eye north of Lindfield. Built with boat access to the Ouse, its surrounding buildings were estate workers' houses. The local blacksmith works from one of these. Buxshalls has been a residential home

Head up to Church Road from Orchards car park and turn right. Cross Hazelgrove Road and turn right heading left down New England Road. After the shops turn left along Barn Cottage Lane. Cross Hanbury Lane and continue down the path between the houses into Scrase Valley Reserve. After 200 yards turn right at the junction and follow the Scrase stream on your left. Exit the Reserve into Croxton Lane, keeping the stream to your left, and cross the bridge on the advertised public footpath into Meadow Drive. Cross the Drive to continue on the footpath opposite which leads into Lindfield Common. Walk across the field aiming in between the seats off Lewes Road. Cross ditch and road to enter Eastern Road turning left up Luxford Road and then Barncroft Drive. As the Drive veers right turn left into the footpath. Continue straight ahead with a large field on your left until the T at a fence. Turn left down the path to All Saints. Turn left before the Church passing through the Churchyard to the High Street. Cross this and continue right out of the village turning left into Spring Lane. Continue respectfully through the grounds of Fulling Mill Farm through the farmyard gate to the footbridge below. Follow signs through the copse and ascend to the right of a large field to the road. Turn right past Buxshalls House and Courtyard, continuing to the main road. Turn left, then right into the road to Horsted Keynes. At the T turn right continuing on the road to another T where you turn left. Shortly after the double bend take the footpath on the right by a metal gate descending alongside the vineyard to the wood. At the T turn right to walk through Paxhill Park estate. Head left along the footpath down the meadow continuing to the road. Turn left to walk to the bridge over the River Ouse. Cross the road continuing by footpath then pavement into Lindfield High Street. Turn right onto the footpath opposite The Tiger beside the Bower House. Walk on past the Vicarage to Hickmans Lane and cross into the Recreation Ground. Head past the left side of the pavilion to the willow trees and the cutting behind them into Pickers Green. Go straight past the roundabout to the end of the road, turning right down the footpath into Hickmans Lane.

Cross into Sunte Avenue continuing to the roundabout and enter the footpath to Old Wickham Lane, from where you turn left into Wickham Way, descending to College Road with St Wilfrid's on the horizon. Cross College Road, turn right and immediately left up Mill Green Road ascending to the roundabout and beyond it. Head left through the car park to the Cricket Pavilion and continue right on the path through the ancient heath to Heath Road. Cross the road and continue along the footpath, next to the car park into Church Road and then into Orchards car park.

8.9 mile/14.3 km

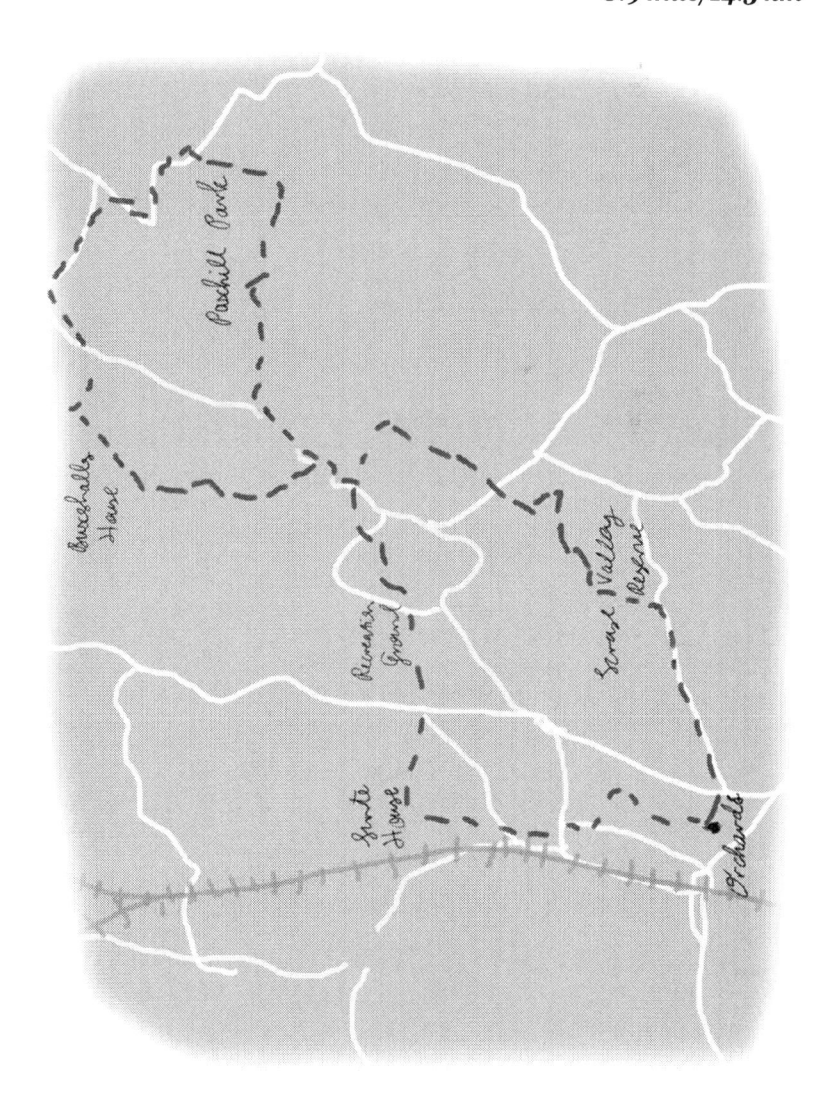

Plumpton Racecourse

> 9 mile walk to Plumpton Racecourse via Wivelsfield Green and Streat returning by bus or train

Old minds are like old horses; you must exercise them if you wish to keep them in working order. John Quincy Adams

Heading south to the Downs through country lanes accessed to the east of Haywards Heath takes you via Streat to Plumpton Racecourse otherwise reached directly by rail from the west of the town, travelling due south then south east after Wivelsfield station. This walk takes you on the former north-south Roman Road to Streat, a straight road fairly safe for walkers. Plumpton Racecourse dates back to 1884. It is a National Hunt or jumping horse-racing course situated south of Plumpton Green and north of Plumpton College which nestles at the bottom of the South Downs. The racecourse is a hilly, tight circuit and has a parallel hurdle course sharing the same uphill finish adding to the drama on race days. Being adjacent to Plumpton railway station with hourly trains from London Victoria to Lewes makes a day at Plumpton races an attractive proposition for Londoners.

From Orchards car park descend through the precinct and turn left along South Road. Continue down to the roundabout and turn left down Caxton Way, continuing straight ahead down the Syresham Gardens footpath beside the stream to St Augustine's Way. Turn right then left along Priory Way to Western Road. Turn left and cross the road into the footpath down to the left of the Cemetery gates. Continue left at the bottom of the graveyard then right into Silver Birches, left into The Hollow and walk on to No. 2. Go up the track to Gravelye Lane and cross diagonally, in effect, to enter Lyoth Lane. Continue up the steep narrow road to Snowdrop Lane, turn right and walk to Lewes Road. Cross the road with care. Turn left along the path and verge, turning right after a distance into Slugwash Lane continuing down to Wivelsfield Green. Turn left at the main road then after a short distance right along the bridle path. Continue to the road at Coldharbour Nursery turning right along Hundred Acre Lane. At the T junction turn left onto Middleton Common Lane and then right shortly afterwards down Streat Lane to Streat. In Streat take the bridle path on your left to Plumpton Racecourse. Turn left just before the Racecourse and follow the perimeter footpath up to Platform 1 of Plumpton Station. Catch the train back to Haywards Heath or the 166 bus to Orchards.

9.2 mile/14.7 km

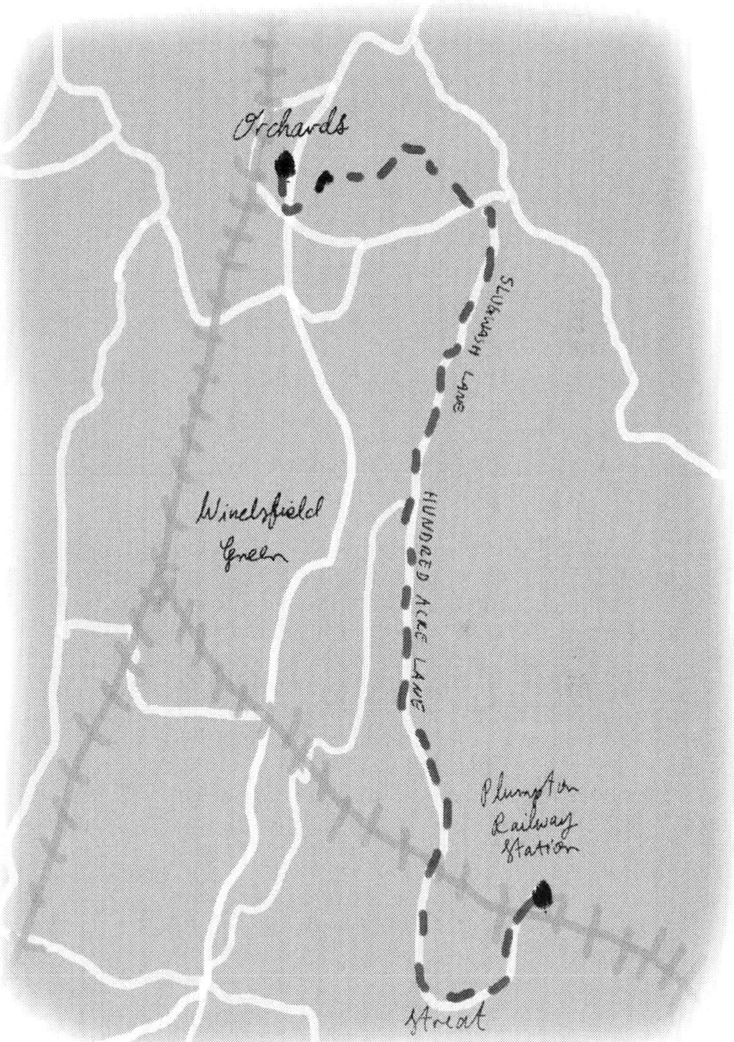
Orchards
SLUGWASH LANE
Wivelsfield Green
HUNDRED ACRE LANE
Plumpton Railway Station
Streat

45   Ashdown Forest

10 mile walk to Ashdown Forest returning by bus

Wherever I am, there's always Pooh, there's always Pooh and Me. Whatever I do, he wants to do, "Where are you going today?" says Pooh.
A.A.Milne

Ashdown Forest on the High Weald is famed for scenic views of North and South Downs. Its hunting drew King Henry VIII when courting Ann Boleyn at Hever Castle. Today people flock here from as far as Japan to play the game of Poohsticks at Pooh Bridge, dropping sticks on the upstream side, with the one whose stick first appears on the downstream side of the bridge being the winner. Winnie-the-Pooh story author A. A. Milne lived on the edge of the forest and took Christopher Robin, his son, walking here. Poohsticks is mentioned in 'The House at Pooh Corner'. A Disney reimagined Pooh Bridge in the forest attracts many.

Head up to Church Road from Orchards car park and turn right. Cross Hazelgrove Road and turn right heading left down New England Road. After the shops turn left along Barn Cottage Lane. Cross Hanbury Lane and continue down the path between the houses into Scrase Valley Reserve. After 200 yards turn right at the junction and follow the Scrase stream on your left. Exit the Reserve into Croxton Lane keeping the stream to your left, and cross the bridge into and then across Meadow Drive, entering the footpath opposite leading into Lindfield Common. Walk across the field aiming in between the seats off Lewes Road. Cross ditch and road to enter Eastern Road turning left up Luxford Road and then Barncroft Drive. As the Drive veers right turn left into the footpath. Continue straight ahead with a large field on your left until the T at a fence. Turn right and continue in the same direction, ignoring the right turn, crossing two stiles before walking along the River Ouse on your left to the road. Turn left walking past East Mascalls Farm and the Paxhill Park Golf Course to the wood. Leave the road ascending the path to your right leading into a large field. Cross the field back to the road along which the path continues briefly to Cockhaise Farm. Turn left here along a track. Take a half right turn along a footpath which descends to cross Bluebell Railway and then skirts below Tremaines Manor to the road. Turn left and walk into Horsted Keynes taking a right turn along Lewes Road. At the T go down through the cutting from the village green into Church Lane. Continue past St Giles onto the bridle path beside the lakes to Broadhurst Manor. Walk straight ahead between the pond and the front of the Manor to Broadhurst Manor Road. Turn right and continue taking another right into Birchgrove Lane. Take the footpath on the left, crossing the stream, continuing to the right of Twyford House and grounds, through woods to join Twyford Lane. Take a left turn and continue to the appropriately named Hindleap Lane beside Ashdown Forest.

Turn right along the road which joins the A22 at Wych Cross. Catch the Orchards 270 bus in front of the Roebuck Hotel.

9.5 mile/15.3 km

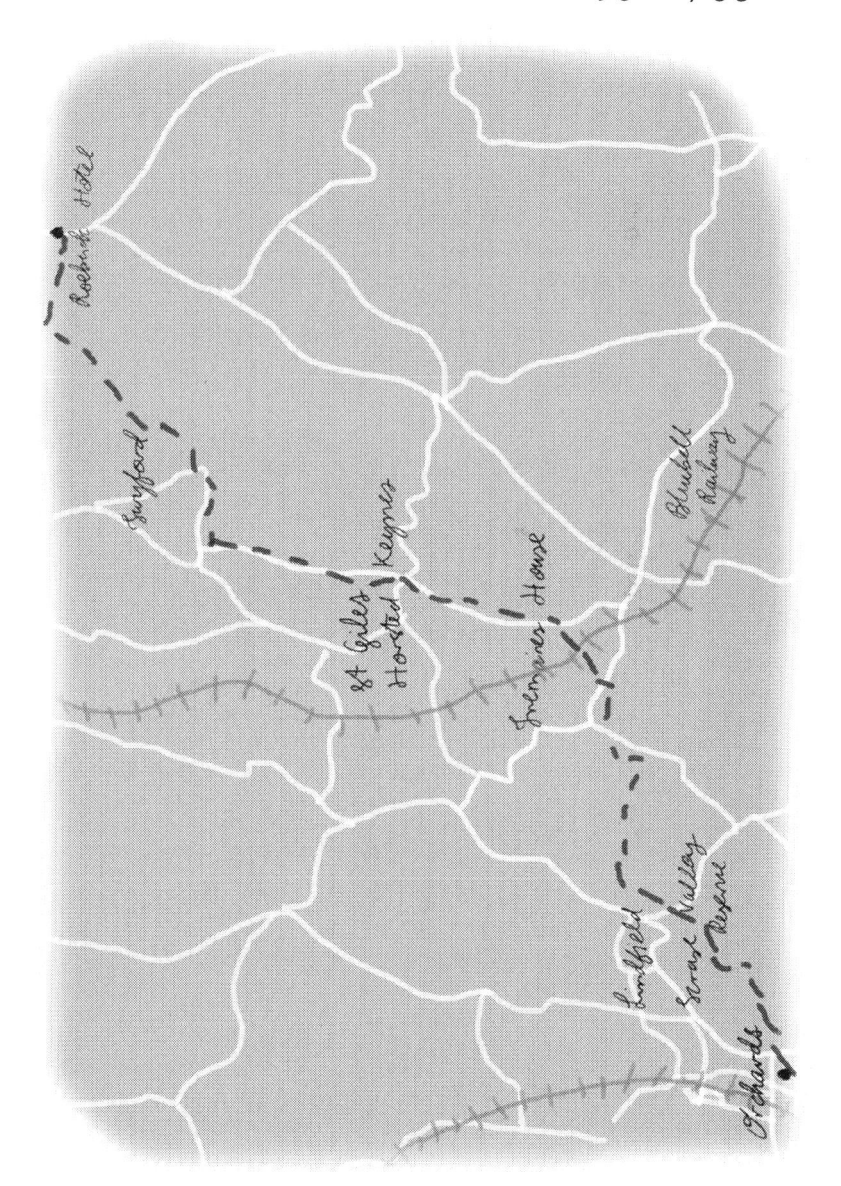

East Grinstead

> 10 mile walk via Ardingly College, Highbrook and Weir Wood to East Grinstead returning by bus

Ye who now will bless the poor shall yourselves find blessing.
John Mason Neale

East Grinstead is on the map of religion, with Protestant martyrs, Anglocatholic pioneers John Mason Neale and the Sisters of St Margaret, Mormons, Scientologists and pagan links to Ashdown Forest. A TV documentary 'Why East Grinstead?' (1994) looked into this with explanations ranging from the presence of ley lines to the idea religious folk were drawn here because of the views! Neale is famous for writing 'Good King Wenceslas' and building the almshouses at Sackville College with scenic views of Ashdown Forest. The High Street has awesome 14th-century timber-framed buildings.

From Orchards car park go up to Church Road and turn right. Cross Hazelgrove Road and turn right heading left down New England Road. After the shops turn left along Barn Cottage. Cross Hanbury Lane continuing between the houses into Scrase Valley Reserve. Turn right at the junction and follow the stream on your left continuing into Croxton Lane and then across the bridge into Meadow Drive. Cross the Drive and continue into Lindfield Common. Continue diagonally across the field to enter Lindfield High Street. Head past All Saints Church and turn left before the right bend entering the footpath running behind the houses to Finches Lane. Turn right and follow the track through the woods to a junction with the road into Kenwards Farm. Turn left to the main road and cross into the wood straight up the path which follows the edge of the field then zig zags through the trees. Turn right at the fork, then right again at a second fork which veers left, continuing on the old railway embankment near Copyhold Lane. At its end descend carefully to the footpath and go through the gate on your right. Cross the Lane diagonally to your right, into the footpath to River's Wood. Cross the stream and follow the steep path upwards, then half right through a field, and the Reservoir comes into sight. Turn right on arrival at the Activity Centre, heading to the water works, and turn left. At the top of the road turn left at the standing footpath sign, past Ardingly Pre-Prep School. Turn right at the grass island heading up to the main school, following the road in front of St Saviour's Chapel to the main entrance. Cross the road, passing through the sports facilities into the wood. Continue straight ahead, out of the wood to the footpath junction sign and continue straight ahead, going over the stile behind it, walking alongside the wood before entering it at the next stile. Follow the well worn path, alert to low branches, over a stream and up into a field.

The path at the field top goes through a long yard into an access road passing Lywood House to the B2028. Cross the road continuing left past Railway Cottages to Burstowhill Lane signed for Highbrook. Walk down the lane bearing left at the Horsted Keynes junction. Continue up past All Saints Church, Highbrook and turn right into Sharpthorne village at the triple road junction. Continue in the same direction out of the village and take a left turn into Grinstead Lane which continues to Weir Wood Reservoir. The road continues across the bridge, becoming West Hoathly Road, passing the Scientology HQ and National Trust's property at Standen, into East Grinstead where you catch the 270 Orchards bus from Sackville College.

9.6 mile/15.4 km

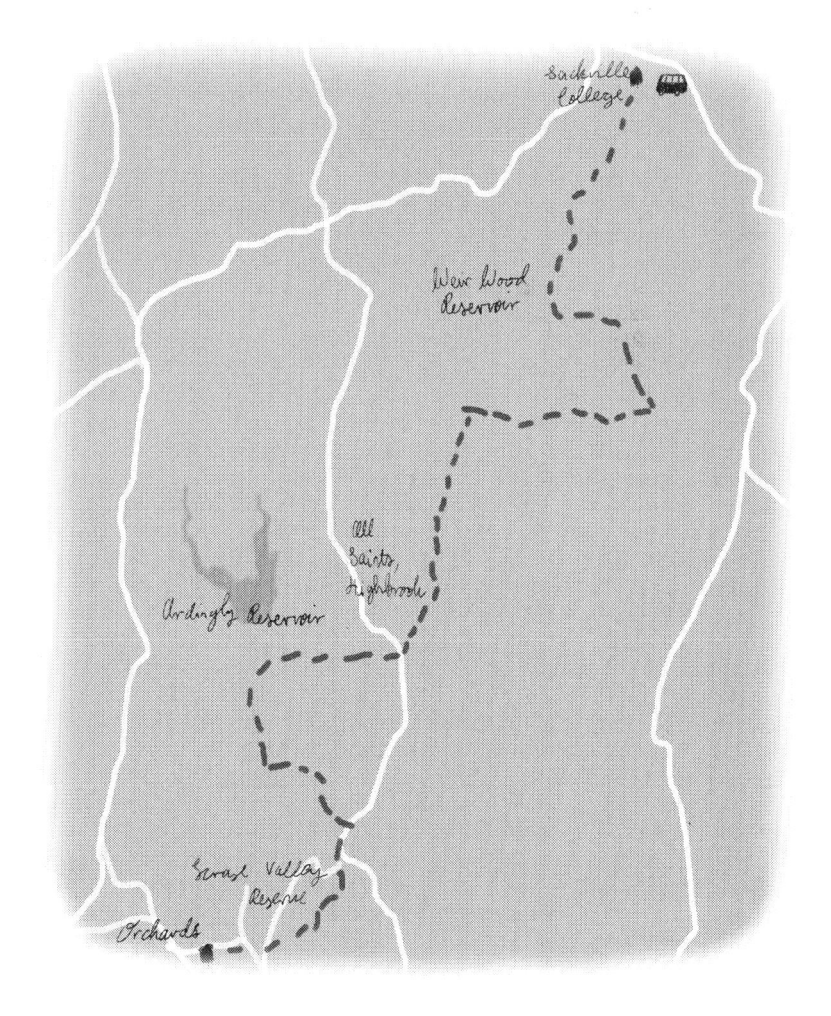

Ardingly

10 mile circular walk to Ardingly

I ask not to see. I ask not to know. I ask simply to be used.
John Henry Newman

Ardingly (pronounced Arding-lye) four miles north of Haywards Heath shares the town's strategic location at the heart of Sussex through its famous showground with capacity to bring thousands of people together as in the South of England Agricultural Show, TV featured Antiques Fairs and global gatherings of Scouts and Guides.

From Orchards car park head up to Church Road and turn right. Cross Hazelgrove Road and turn right, heading left down New England Road. After the shops turn left along Barn Cottage Lane. Cross Hanbury Lane and continue between the houses into Scrase Valley Reserve. Turn right at the junction and follow the Scrase stream on your left. Exit the Reserve into Croxton Lane crossing the bridge on the footpath into Meadow Drive. Cross the Drive to continue into Lindfield Common. Walk across the field aiming in between the seats off Lewes Road. Cross ditch and road to enter Eastern Road, turning left up Luxford Road and then Barncroft Drive. As the Drive veers right, turn left into the footpath. Continue straight ahead with a large field on your left until the T at a fence. Turn left down the path to All Saints. Turn left before the Church, passing through the Churchyard to the High Street. Cross this and continue right out of the village, turning left into Spring Lane. Continue respectfully through the grounds of Fulling Mill Farm, through the farmyard gate to the footbridge below. Follow signs through the copse and ascend to the right of a large field to the road. Turn left at the road, walking up to Hill House Farm gate and follow the footpath to the left of this. Pass through a gate, after which the track narrows to a covered footpath. Keep straight ahead at the junction, continuing along the permissive footpath, across a stream and up the steps of the old railway embankment. Continue right along the track, then as signed, down to the left. Turn right then immediately left, as signed, to follow the path out of the wood. Continue on the path up through the fields, into the hedged path to the houses, following the track to the main road. Turn left along the pavement and head straight across, into Street Lane to St Peter's Church and left along Church Lane. Take the right path down the fields and cross the stile into the waterside path. Turn left and continue through the loving gate, along the main reservoir bank heading up the path on the grassy bank ahead. Continue left through a metal gate and up the field to the left of the copse. Continue left down the field. At the bottom, cross a bridge then head to cross a second bridge and into Rivers Wood, proceeding on the footpath up to Copyhold Lane. Cross diagonally to your right to join the footpath signed by the gate.

Head up, then turn right along the edge of Haywards Heath Golf Course, following the footpath signs straight ahead which take you into a covered path, ascending to the walls of Wickham Farm. Turn right and then left down Wickham Way to College Road. Cross, turn right and immediately left up Mill Green Road, up to the roundabout and beyond. Head left through the car park round the Cricket Pavilion up through the heath to Heath Road. Cross and follow the footpath into Church Road and then back into Orchards car park.

10.3 mile/16.6 km

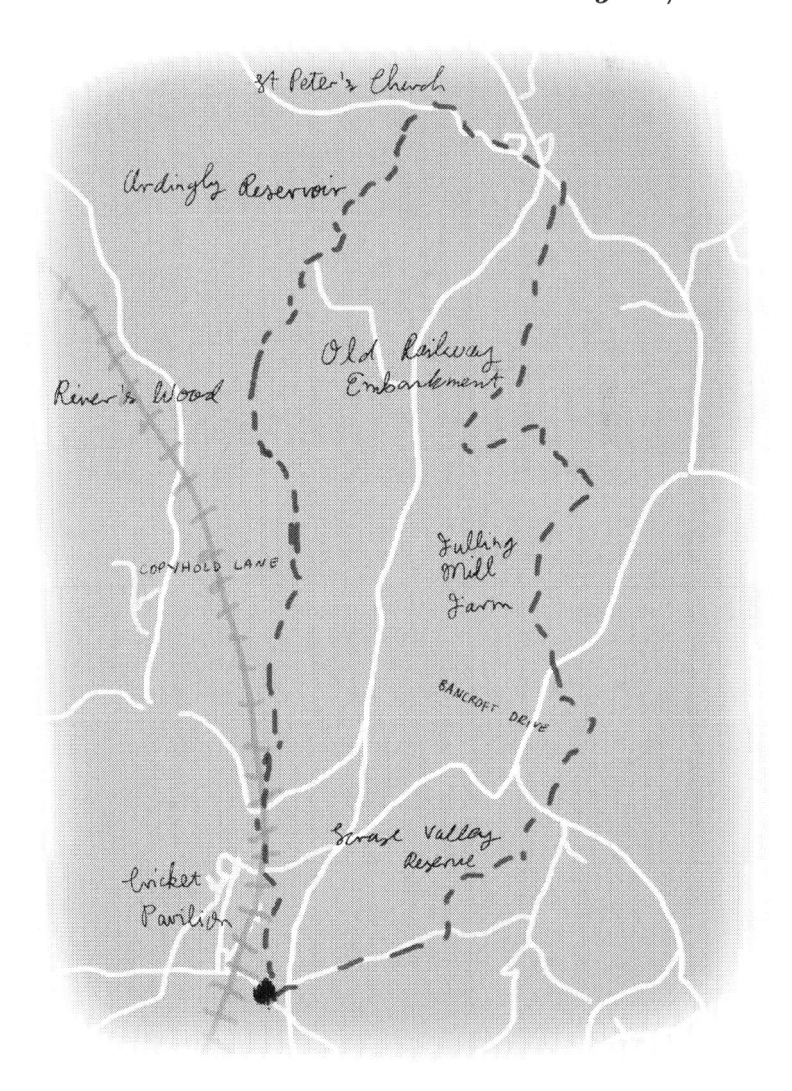

Jack & Jill

> 11 mile walk to Jack & Jill windmills returning by bus

Up from the hollow and on to the Hill, the long gaunt Hill that slopes from the sea, with grey green curves and never a tree, and the Dewpond lying round and still. Amy Sawyer

The Dewpond in Amy Sawyer's poem 'On the Sussex Downs' might be one of two immediately accessed by turning left from the Sussex Border Path (SBP) at the summit of the Downs from Ditchling, rather than right on this walk to Jack & Jill windmills. Artificial ponds help keep livestock on water permeable chalk limestone. Since 1821 Jill then Jack windmill have profited from the Downs' more plentiful resource of wind.

Descend the precinct from Orchards car park and turn left along South Road. Continue down to the roundabout and turn left down Caxton Way continuing straight ahead down the Syresham Gardens footpath beside the stream to St Augustine's Way. Turn right then left along Priory Way to Western Road. Turn left and cross the road into the footpath, down to the left of the Cemetery gates. Continue left at the bottom of the graveyard, then right into Silver Birches, left into The Hollow and walk on to No. 2. Go up the track to Gravelye Lane and cross diagonally, in effect to enter Lyoth Lane. Continue up the steep narrow road to Snowdrop Lane, turn right and walk to Lewes Road. Cross the road carefully. Turn left along the path and verge, turning right after a distance into Slugwash Lane, descending to Wivelsfield Green where you cross the main road into Eastern Road opposite. Continue past the village hall round the right bend and left as signed along the lane before the houses. At the end of this lane enter the bridleway through West Wood ignoring paths to right or left aided by SBP signs. Exit onto a track with houses continuing to the road. Turn right crossing at the top of Spatham Lane into the footpath and along the edge of a field. After a gate, turn left over a stile into a large field, heading left to cross the railway. Take the path on the left down the field, crossing stiles into a copse, following the path into a field. Continue down over a bridge bearing right along the path, then left through the stile into a narrow path which opens into a field. Continue over two stiles into another narrow path opening into a field. Go through a wooden gate to a sign posted 'dog leg' in the path, left then right. Continue past the pond to a stile and on to rejoin SBP. Go straight ahead through two farm gates past Mac's Farm across a lane then over a stile followed by a right turn over a stile into a field crossing left to climb over another stile. Head right, passing through two gates, left down East Gardens and left into Ditchling. SBP continues south through the village and is signed to the right of the left turn into Beacon Road.

At the top of this fenced path turn right following SBP across the fields. Continue to the left of a vineyard to Underhill Lane. Turn right and shortly left following SBP signs up the Downs. Look back towards Haywards Heath's old hospital with the windmill at Keymer in the foreground. Go through the gate at the top of the Downs. Turn right continuing on the South Downs Way before descending right to Jack & Jill windmills. Continue down the road and cross walking left to the Riding School entrance to catch a 270 or 272 bus to Orchards.

11.4 mile/18.3 km

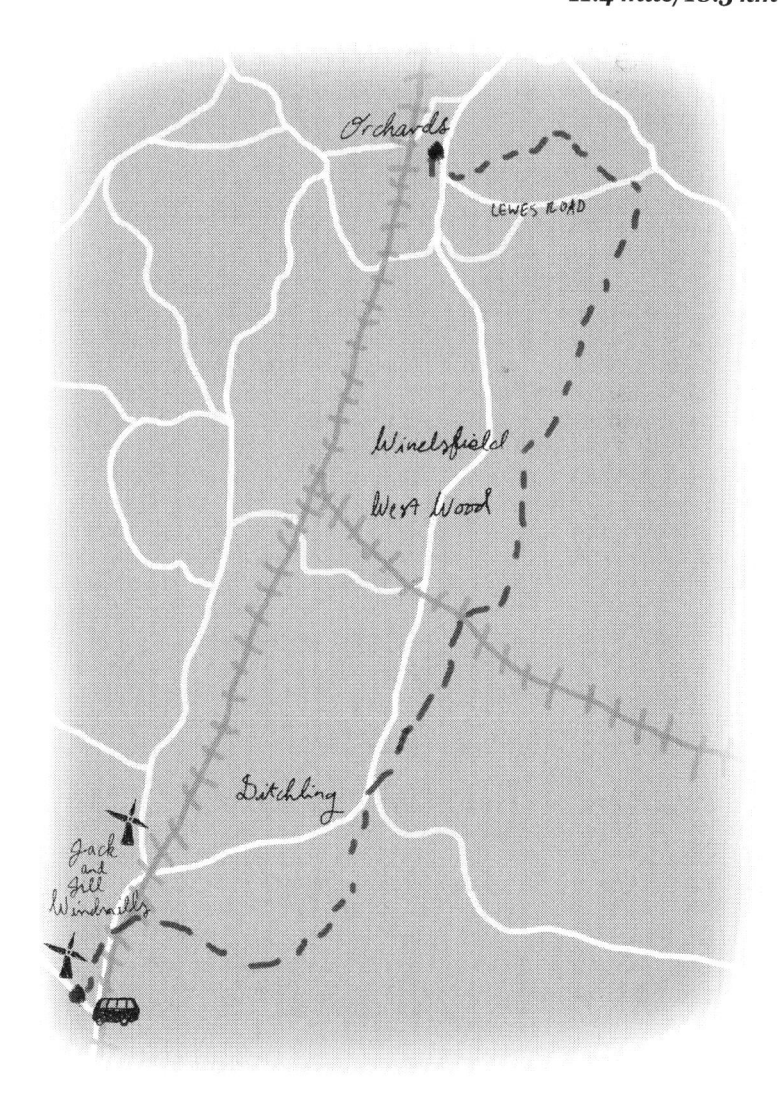

Brighton

> 13 mile walk to Patcham in north Brighton following the Sussex Border Path through Ditchling and past the Chattri memorial returning by bus

What cliffs are there, what bracing air, what hills to fly a kite on! What cricket grounds, what packs of hounds, to tempt the lads of Brighton!
Charles Hervey

Go down the precinct from Orchards car park and turn left along South Road. Continue down to the roundabout and turn left down Caxton Way continuing straight ahead down the Syresham Gardens footpath beside the stream to St Augustine's Way. Turn right then left along Priory Way to Western Road. Turn left and cross the road into the footpath down to the left of the Cemetery gates. Continue left at the bottom of the graveyard then right into Silver Birches, left into The Hollow and walk on to No. 2. Go up the track to Gravelye Lane and cross diagonally in effect to enter Lyoth Lane. Continue up the steep narrow road to Snowdrop Lane, turn right and walk to Lewes Road. Cross the road. Turn left to walk carefully along the path and verge, turning right after a distance into Slugwash Lane descending to Wivelsfield Green where you cross the main road into Eastern Road opposite. Continue past the village hall round the right bend and left as signed along the lane before the houses. At the end of this lane enter the bridleway through West Wood ignoring paths to right or left aided by Sussex Border Path (SBP) signs. Exit onto a track with houses continuing to the road. Turn right crossing at the top of Spatham Lane into the footpath along the edge of a field. After a gate, turn left over a stile into a large field, heading left to cross the railway. Take the path on the left down the field crossing stiles into a copse following the path into a field. Continue down over a bridge, bearing right along the path, then left through the stile, into a narrow path which opens into a field. Continue over two stiles into another narrow path opening into a field. Go through a wooden gate to a sign posted 'dog leg' in the path, left then right. Continue past the pond to a stile and on to rejoin SBP. Go straight ahead through two farm gates, past Mac's Farm, across a lane then over a stile, followed by a right turn over a stile into a field, crossing left to climb over another stile. Head right, passing through two gates, left down East Gardens and left into Ditchling. SBP continues south through the village and is signed to the right of the left turn into Beacon Road. At the top of the fenced path turn right, following SBP across the fields and to the left of a vineyard to Underhill Lane. Turn right and shortly left following SBP signs up the Downs. Go through the gate at the top of the Downs, turning right along the South Downs Way through the gate, then turn left down the path through fields following SBP signs. Brighton's i360 looms ahead on the horizon, the radio station masts above Glynde to the far left and above Fulking to the far right.

Further down Jack & Jill windmills appear to the right. At the footpath crossing continue straight ahead through the gate. Shortly after the copse the Chattri (1921) appears to the left of your descent. This is a memorial to Hindu and Sikh Indian soldiers, previously hospitalised in Brighton's Dome, who died and were cremated here on the Downs. Continuing down from the Chattri, keep straight heading for i360 on the horizon. Pass through the gate under the electric wires as the hum of traffic ascends from the A27. At the car park turn right along the road and follow the pavement round. Cross the A27 slip road to the left of the grassed roundabout heading for the Lewes sign. Continue on the pavement across the A27 bridge, and after the roundabout follow left, then cross the slip road, turning right. On the pavement, continue left into Vale Avenue. Take the first right walking past All Saints Church through Patcham to Brighton's London Road. Cross to catch a 270 or 272 back to Haywards Heath.

13 mile/20.9 km

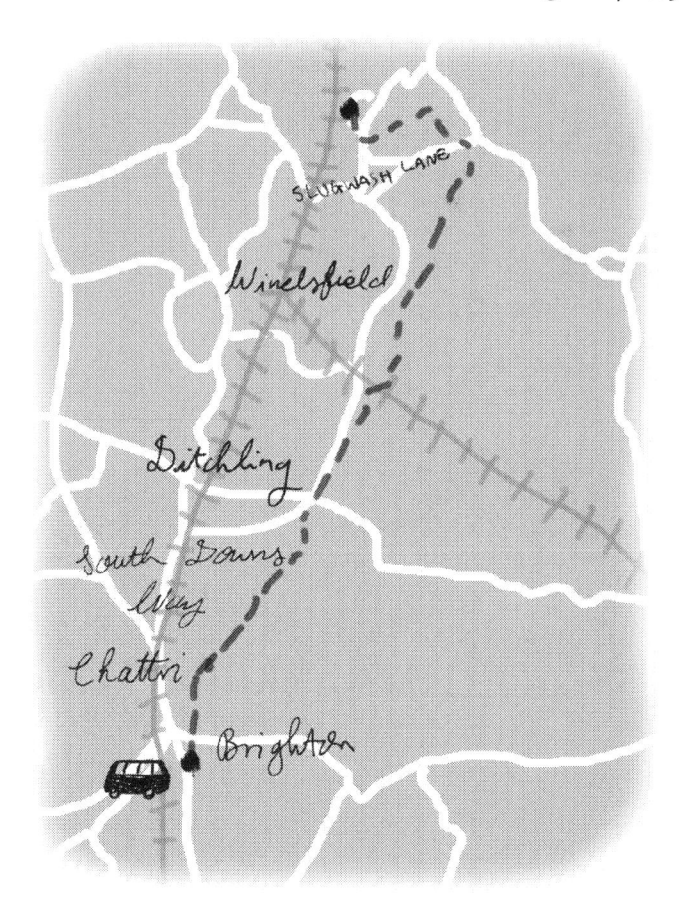

Lewes

> 13 mile walk via Wivelsfield Green and Streat Hill to the South Downs continuing to Lewes returning by bus

All is silent now, silent the bell that, heard from yonder ivy'd turret high, warned the cowled brother from his midnight cell, silent the vesper chant - the Litany. W.L.Bowles on Lewes Priory

East Sussex County town, Lewes meaning 'hills' in Old English, takes its name from its setting. Situated on the River Ouse it was an important port until Newhaven gained prominence with the advent of the railway. Lewes Castle stands above the town and the ruins of St Pancras Priory (1081) below it. Between 1555 -1557 seventeen Protestant martyrs were burned at the stake, which is vigorously commemorated on November 5th. This walk reverses a possible route from Lewes by Puritan soldiers to the battle of Haywards Heath (1642) for successful conflict with Royalist troops.

Go down the shopping precinct from Orchards car park and turn left along South Road. Continue down to the roundabout and turn left down Caxton Way, continuing straight ahead down the Syresham Gardens footpath beside the stream to St Augustine's Way. Turn right then left along Priory Way to Western Road. Turn left and cross the road into the footpath down to the left of the Cemetery gates. Continue left at the bottom of the graveyard then right into Silver Birches, left into The Hollow and walk on to No. 2. Go up the track to Gravelye Lane and cross diagonally, in effect, to enter Lyoth Lane. Continue up the steep narrow road to Snowdrop Lane, turn right and walk to Lewes Road. Cross the road carefully. Turn left to walk along the path and verge turning right after a distance into Slugwash Lane, continuing down to Wivelsfield Green. Turn left at the main road, then after a short distance right along the bridle path. Continue to the road at Coldharbour Nursery, turning right along Hundred Acre Lane. At the T junction turn left onto Middleton Common Lane and then right shortly afterwards down Streat Lane to Streat continuing south to B2116. Turn left, then right, up the lane signed to Streat Hill Farm House. Take the Streat Hill footpath on your left or gentler road ascent. The path rejoins the road for the last ascent to the South Downs Way sign. Turn left, continuing straight ahead at the Black Cap crossing. Take the lower right hand footpath below Mount Harry, heading down to walk on the left of the old Lewes Racecourse. Follow the footpath to the left before the stables entrance. Cross Race Hill road and the stile on the other side. Head half left on the path down to the stile giving access to Firle Crescent, Lewes. Turn right continuing to Nevill Road (A275) and right again to catch the 166 Orchards bus at the junction with Nevill Crescent.

13.1 mile/21.1 km

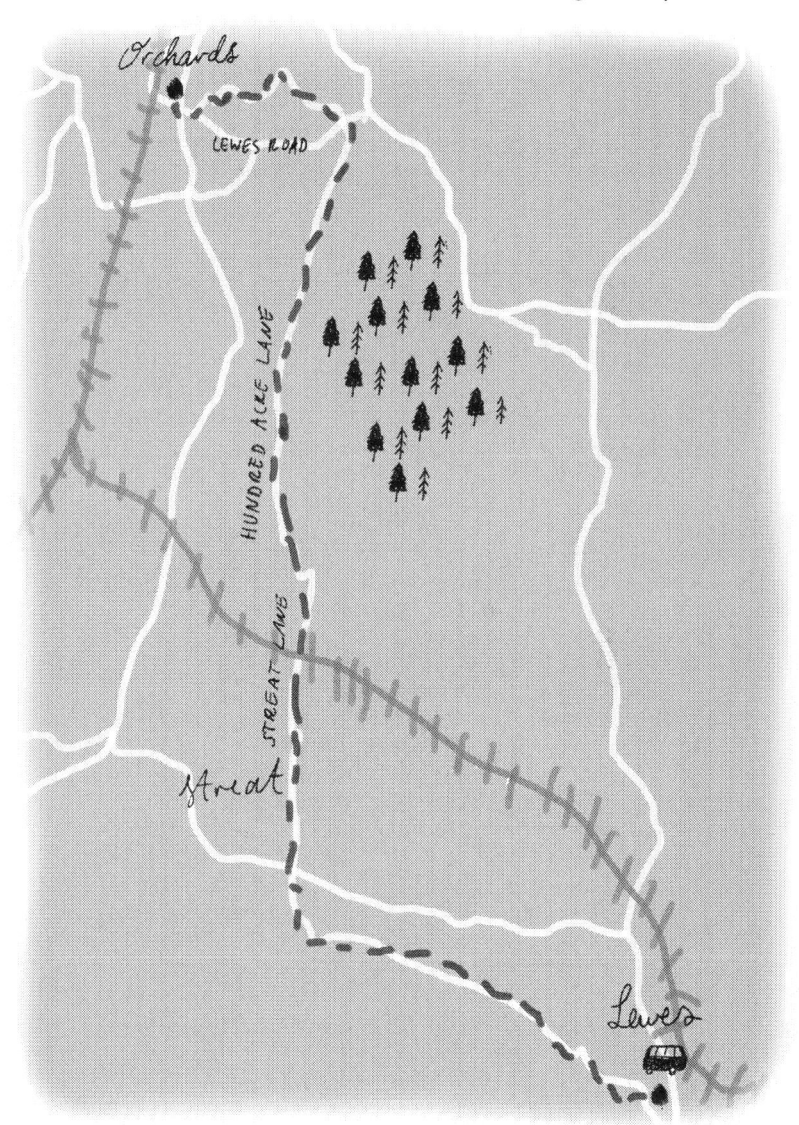

Orchards

LEWES ROAD

HUNDRED ACRE LANE

STREAT LANE

Streat

Lewes

Notes

1. http://www.theorchardsshopping.com/
2. Colin Manton, *Haywards Heath Through Time* (Amberley, 2013), Kindle location 110
3. Colin Manton, *Haywards Heath Through Time*, location 163
4. Wyn K Ford & AC Gabe, *The Metropolis of Mid Sussex - A History of Haywards Heath* (Charles Clarke, 1981), p147-9
5. Jess Bauldry, *The Argus* (31 January 2008)
6. Ford & Gabe, *Metropolis of Mid Sussex*, p140
7. Peter Miles, communication to the author
8. Hanna Prince, *The People who shaped Haywards Heath* (Sussex Living, September 2019), *p57*
9. Hanna Prince, *People who shaped Haywards Heath,* p51-53
10. https://www.bsuh.nhs.uk/hospitals/princess-royal-hospital/
11. Richard Bryant, note to author on Lindfield Inns & Alehouses
12. The Revd Ray Smith, communication to the author on Ascension Church
13. Vera Arlett, *Another Book of Sussex Verse* edited C.F.Cook (Hove, Sussex Combridges,1928) p4
14. Lilian Rogers, *Haywards Heath - yesterday remembered* (Lilian Rogers, 1999), p30
15. Colin Manton, *Haywards Heath Through Time*, location 645
16. Alice Cooke, *Sussex Life* (November 2013)
17. Ford & Gabe, *Metropolis of Mid Sussex,* p3
18. Margaret Nicolle, *William Allen, Quaker Friend of Lindfield 1770-1843* (Margaret Nicolle, 2001)
19. David Jamieson, *Old Cuckfield* (Stenlake Publishing, 2017), p3
20. Ford & Gabe, *Metropolis of Mid Sussex,* p85
21. https://en.wikipedia.org/wiki/A272_road
22. https://en.wikipedia.org/wiki/Wivelsfield
23. https://en.wikipedia.org/wiki/Ansty,_West_Sussex
24. Hilaire Belloc, *Book of Sussex Verse* edited C.F.Cook (Hove, Sussex Combridges, 1914), p6
25. https://en.wikipedia.org/wiki/Abbots_Leigh
26. Canon John Twisleton, *A History of St Giles Church, Horsted Keynes* (St Giles Church, 2015), p18-23, p27-28
27. https://en.wikipedia.org/wiki/High_Weald_Landscape_Trail
28. Peter Duncan, Gwyn Mansfield & Brian Tester, *Lindfield Remembered* (SB Publications, 2002)
29. West Sussex County Council et al *Ardingly Amble* (1999) on the abandoned Ouse Valley railway embankment off Copyhold Lane
30. Victor Neuburg, *Another Book of Sussex Verse,* p152
31. https://en.wikipedia.org/wiki/Walstead
32. https://en.wikipedia.org/wiki/Ardingly_College
33. https://en.wikipedia.org/wiki/Wakehurst_Place
34. West Sussex County Council et al *Ardingly Amble* on Ardingly Reservoir
35. John Twisleton, *Pointers to Heaven* (Amazon, 2020), p24

36	West Sussex County Council et al *Ardingly Amble* on Balcombe viaduct
37	https://en.wikipedia.org/wiki/Ditchling
38	https://en.wikipedia.org/wiki/High_Weald_Landscape_Trail
39	John Galsworthy, *The Book of Sussex Verse*, p114
40	Canon John Twisleton, *A History of St Giles Church, Horsted Keynes*, p27-28
41	https://amnesiainternational.net/en/paxhill-parka-historical-insight-mansions-inhabitants-etc
42	https://sussexparishchurches.org/church/wivelsfield-st-peter-and-st-john-the-baptist/
43	https://www.parksandgardens.org/places/buxshalls
44	https://en.wikipedia.org/wiki/Plumpton_Racecourse
45	https://en.wikipedia.org/wiki/Ashdown_Forest
46	https://en.wikipedia.org/wiki/East_Grinstead
47	https://en.wikipedia.org/wiki/South_of_England_Show
48	Amy Sawyer, *Another Book of Sussex Verse*, p189
49	https://en.wikipedia.org/wiki/Brighton
50	https://en.wikipedia.org/wiki/Lewes

About the author

John Twisleton is an ideas and people person, writer and broadcaster. He lives in Haywards Heath with involvements in London and Brighton. A Yorkshireman living in Sussex he now sees himself as much a Downsman as a Dalesman and is committed to lowering carbon footprints through recreational use of footpaths and public transport. He has published books on Horsted Keynes and prayer and is author of the popular 'Forty Walks from Ally Pally'

Printed in Great Britain
by Amazon